Linux Command Line Mastery

A Comprehensive Guide for

Beginners and Beyond

By

Noah Aerav

Table of Contents

Introduction

Welcome to the dynamic world of command-line mastery and shell scripting! In this comprehensive book, we embark on a journey to unlock the full potential of the command line interface (CLI) and delve deep into the art of scripting with Bash.

Why This Book?

If you've ever felt daunted by the blinking cursor of a terminal or struggled to automate tasks efficiently, fear not! This book is your roadmap to command-line proficiency and scripting expertise. Whether you're a novice looking to harness the power of the command line or an experienced user seeking advanced scripting techniques, you'll find a wealth of knowledge within these pages.

What You'll Learn

Starting with the fundamentals, we'll guide you through essential commands, file manipulation, and understanding file permissions. You'll master the art of text manipulation, from simple pipelines to complex regular expressions. Then, we'll dive into the world of Bash scripting, teaching you how to automate tasks, handle logic and loops, work with arrays, and debug with finesse.

Interactive Learning

Throughout the book, you'll find hands-on examples, practical exercises, and real-world scenarios to reinforce your learning. Each chapter builds upon the previous one, ensuring a gradual and comprehensive understanding of the command line and scripting concepts.

Who Is This Book For?

- **Beginners**: If you're new to the command line, this book provides a gentle yet thorough introduction, guiding you from basic commands to scripting proficiency.

- **Intermediate Users**: For those already familiar with the command line, you'll find a wealth of intermediate and advanced topics to deepen your skills and streamline your workflow.

- **System Administrators**: Learn essential techniques for managing permissions, automating tasks, and troubleshooting scripts like a pro.

Let's Begin!

Part I:
Command Line
Fundamentals

Chapter 1:
Terminal Tamers

Picture this: you're seated before a computer, fingers poised above the keyboard, ready to embark on a digital adventure. But instead of the familiar landscape of icons and windows, you're faced with a stark black screen and a blinking cursor. This, my fellow explorer, is the gateway to the **Linux command line** – a realm of power and efficiency, where cryptic commands become magic spells and your keyboard transforms into a wand of control.

While graphical interfaces offer a friendly facade, the command line grants you direct access to the inner workings of your computer. It's the language spoken by power users, system administrators, and programmers alike. But fear not, for this chapter will be your guide as we take our first steps into this exciting new world. We'll tame the terminal, learn the basic vocabulary of shell commands, and unravel the mysteries of the Linux file system. So, take a deep breath, summon your courage, and let the adventure begin!

1. The Command Line Unveiled

The command line interface (CLI), often referred to as the terminal or simply the shell, is a text-based method of interacting with your computer. Unlike graphical interfaces that rely on clicking icons and navigating menus, the command line allows you to issue commands directly to the operating system using typed instructions. It may seem intimidating at first, but beneath the surface lies a world of power, precision, and efficiency.

Why Embrace the Command Line?

In the age of sleek graphical interfaces, you might wonder why anyone would bother with the seemingly archaic command line. However, seasoned Linux users and professionals swear by its numerous advantages:

- **Power and Flexibility**: The command line offers a vast repertoire of commands and options, allowing you to perform intricate tasks with surgical precision. From managing files and automating system administration tasks to processing data and developing software, the possibilities are limitless.
- **Efficiency and Speed**: Once you grasp the fundamentals, the command line becomes a remarkably efficient way to interact with your computer. Complex operations that would require multiple clicks and menu navigations in a graphical interface can be accomplished with a single, concise command.
- **Scripting and Automation**: The command line allows you to create shell scripts – essentially text files containing a series of commands – to automate repetitive tasks. This saves you time and effort, allowing you to focus on more creative and productive endeavors.
- **Remote Access and Control**: The command line is essential for remotely managing servers and other systems. With tools like SSH, you can securely access and control remote machines from anywhere in the world, as if you were sitting right in front of them.
- **Understanding the System**: By working with the command line, you gain a deeper understanding of the inner workings of your operating system. You'll learn about file systems, processes, permissions, and other fundamental concepts that make your computer tick.

The Shell – Your Command Interpreter

At the heart of the command line experience lies the shell. The shell is a program that acts as an intermediary between you and the operating system. It reads the commands you type and executes them, translating your instructions into actions performed by the kernel and other programs.

The most common shell used in Linux distributions is the Bash shell, which stands for "Bourne Again Shell". It's a powerful and versatile tool, offering a rich set of features for both interactive use and scripting. As we progress through this book, you'll become intimately familiar with Bash and its capabilities, unlocking the true potential of the Linux command line.

2. Terminal Emulators – Your Gateway to the Shell

While the shell is the heart of the command line, we need a way to access it within our graphical desktop environment. This is where **terminal emulators** come in. These handy programs provide a window into the shell, allowing you to interact with it using your keyboard and mouse, just like you would with any other graphical application.

Popular Terminal Emulators in Linux

Several excellent terminal emulators are available for Linux, each offering unique features and customization options. Here are a few of the most popular choices:
- **Konsole (KDE)**: The default terminal emulator for the KDE desktop environment. It boasts a wide array of features, including tabbed interfaces, split views, customizable color schemes, and profile management.
- **Gnome Terminal (Gnome)**: The standard terminal emulator for the Gnome desktop environment. It's known for its simplicity and ease of use, while still offering essential features like multiple tabs and profiles.
- **Xterm**: A classic and lightweight terminal emulator that's been around since the early days of the X Window System. It's a reliable choice for those seeking a no-frills terminal experience.
- **Terminator**: A powerful terminal emulator that allows for multiple terminal sessions within a single window. You can split the window horizontally or vertically and create complex layouts to suit your workflow.
- **Guake**: A drop-down terminal emulator inspired by the Quake console. It hides discreetly at the top of your screen and can be summoned with a single keystroke, making it perfect for quick commands and checks.

Launching a Terminal Emulator

The way you launch a terminal emulator depends on your specific Linux distribution and desktop environment. Generally, you can find it in the applications menu under the "System Tools" or "Utilities" category. You can also often launch it with a keyboard shortcut, such as `Ctrl+Alt+T` in many Gnome-based systems.

Once launched, you'll be greeted with a window displaying the shell prompt. This is your command center, where you'll issue commands and witness the magic of the command line unfold. Take some time to familiarize yourself with the interface, explore the menus and options, and discover the features your chosen terminal emulator offers. You'll find that many of them allow extensive customization, from adjusting fonts and colors to configuring keyboard shortcuts and creating profiles for specific tasks.

3. The Shell Prompt – Your Command Center

The blinking cursor on the black screen might seem like a simple invitation to type, but it represents something much more profound – a gateway to the power of the operating system. This is your **shell prompt**, a visual indicator that the shell is ready and waiting for your commands.

Deciphering the Prompt

While the appearance of the prompt may vary slightly depending on your Linux distribution and configuration, it typically follows a common structure:

```
[noah@linux_lab working_directory]$
```

Let's break down the components of this prompt:
- `[ ]` - Square brackets often enclose the prompt elements.
- `noah` - The username of the currently logged-in user.
- `@` - The at symbol separates the username and hostname.
- `linux_lab` - The hostname of the computer.
- `working_directory` - The current working directory, indicating your location within the file system.
- `$` - The dollar sign is the most common ending for a regular user prompt.

Superuser Status

If you're logged in as the superuser (also known as root), the prompt will typically end with a `#` symbol instead of a `$`. This indicates that you have elevated privileges and can perform administrative tasks that require access to system files and settings.

```
[noah@linux_lab working_directory]#
```

It's important to exercise caution when operating as the superuser, as even a small mistake can have significant consequences for your system's stability and security.

4. First Steps – Basic Shell Commands

With the terminal emulator open and the shell prompt awaiting your command, it's time to take your first steps into the world of the Linux command line. In this section, we'll explore a few fundamental commands that will lay the foundation for your journey. These commands are like your basic tools – a trusty hammer, a reliable screwdriver – that you'll use time and again as you build your command line expertise.

pwd – Revealing Your Current Location

Imagine yourself as an intrepid explorer navigating a vast and intricate jungle. To chart your course and understand your surroundings, you need to know your current location. The pwd command, which stands for "print working directory," serves as your compass in the Linux file system, revealing your exact position within the directory structure.

To use pwd, simply type it at the shell prompt and press Enter:

```
[noah@linux_lab ~]$ pwd
/home/noah
```

The output /home/noah in this example indicates that the current working directory is /home/noah, which is the home directory for the user *noah*. The home directory is your personal space in the Linux file system, where you can create and store your files and directories.

You'll find that pwd is an invaluable tool as you navigate the file system, allowing you to always keep track of where you are and where you're going.

cd – Navigating the File System Like a Pro

Now that you know how to pinpoint your current location with pwd, it's time to learn how to move around. The cd command, short for "change directory," is your vehicle for navigating the hierarchical structure of the Linux file system. With cd, you can jump between directories, explore different branches of the file system tree, and reach your desired destination with ease.

To change your working directory, simply type `cd` followed by the path of the directory you want to move to:

```
[noah@linux_lab ~]$ cd /usr/bin
[noah@linux_lab bin]$
```

In this example, we've navigated from the home directory (~) to the **/usr/bin** directory, which contains many of the system's executable programs. Notice how the prompt changes to reflect your new location?

The `cd` command is versatile and offers several shortcuts to make navigation even more efficient:

Option	Meaning
cd	Typing `cd` without specifying a directory will transport you directly back to your home directory, no matter where you are in the file system. It's like clicking your heels together and saying, "There's no place like home."
cd -	This handy shortcut takes you back to the previous directory you were in, allowing you to quickly switch between two locations.
cd ~username	You can jump directly to another user's home directory by specifying their username after the tilde (~). For example, `cd ~root` would take you to the root user's home directory (typically **/root**).

As you become more familiar with the file system layout and your own workflow, you'll discover the power and flexibility of the `cd` command, making navigation a breeze.

ls – Listing Files and Directories with Style

As you navigate the file system, you'll need a way to see what's inside each directory – the files it contains, the subdirectories it holds. The `ls` command, short for "list", does just that, revealing the contents of directories with various options to customize the display.

In its simplest form, typing `ls` at the shell prompt will list the contents of your current working directory:

```
[noah@linux_lab bin]$ ls
[ 2to3-2.7  411toppm  a2p  ...  zsoelim ]
```

Ah, but `ls` is much more than a simple list generator. It offers a variety of options to enhance its output and provide valuable information about the listed files and directories. Let's explore a few:

Option	Meaning
ls -l	This option displays a detailed list, including file permissions, ownership, size, and modification date. It's like getting a dossier on each file and directory, revealing their attributes and secrets.
ls -a	By default, ls hides files whose names begin with a dot (.), known as hidden files. The -a option reveals these hidden gems, often used for configuration files and application settings.
ls -R	This option delves deeper into the directory structure, listing not only the contents of the specified directory but also the contents of its subdirectories, and their subdirectories, and so on.
ls -h	When used with -l, this option displays file sizes in a human-friendly format (e.g., KB, MB, GB) instead of bytes, making it easier to grasp the magnitude of each file.
ls -S	Sorts the output by file size, with the largest files appearing first.
ls -t	Sorts the output by modification time, with the most recently modified files at the top.
ls -r	Reverses the order of the sort, so you can view files in descending order.

Experiment with these options and discover the many ways `ls` can illuminate the contents of your directories. You'll find that `ls -l` is particularly useful as you learn more about file permissions and ownership in later chapters.

clear – Clearing the Screen for a Fresh Start

As you work with the command line, your terminal window can quickly become cluttered with the output of previous commands, making it difficult to focus on the task at hand. The `clear` command is like a refreshing breeze, instantly clearing the screen and providing a clean slate for your next commands.

Using `clear` is as simple as it gets: just type `clear` at the prompt and press Enter. Poof! The screen is wiped clean, and your prompt appears at the top, ready for action.

```
[noah@linux_lab bin]$ clear
[noah@linux_lab bin]$
```

While it may seem like a minor convenience, `clear` helps maintain a tidy and organized workspace, allowing you to focus on the commands you're typing without distractions from previous output. It's a small but powerful tool for enhancing your command line experience.

5. Pathways and Destinations – Absolute vs. Relative Paths

Just as a map guides you through a city, **paths** help you navigate the intricate structure of the Linux file system. A path is essentially the address of a file or directory, specifying its location within the hierarchical tree. Understanding paths is crucial for effectively using the command line, and there are two main types of paths you'll encounter: **absolute paths** and **relative paths**.

Absolute Paths – Starting from the Root

An **absolute path** is like a complete street address – it provides the full and unambiguous location of a file or directory, starting from the root directory (denoted by /) and traversing the directory tree branch by branch.

For example, the absolute path `/usr/bin/zip` indicates the following:

- Start at the root directory (/).
- Move to the `usr` directory.
- Within `usr`, navigate to the `bin` directory.
- Finally, locate the file named `zip` within the `bin` directory.

Absolute paths always start with the root directory and leave no room for ambiguity. They are particularly useful when you need to specify the exact location of a file or directory, regardless of your current working directory.

Relative Paths – Navigating from Your Current Location

A **relative path** is like giving directions based on your current location. It specifies the location of a file or directory relative to your current working directory, eliminating the need to start from the root each time.

Relative paths use two special symbols to denote positions within the file system:

- **. (dot)**: Represents the current working directory.

- **.. (dot dot)**: Represents the parent directory, one level above your current location.

For example, if your current working directory is `/home/noah`, the following relative paths would point to these locations:

- `Documents`: Refers to the `Documents` directory within your home directory, equivalent to the absolute path `/home/noah/Documents`.
- `../Downloads`: Refers to the `Downloads` directory, which is located in the parent directory of your home directory.
- `./bin/myscript`: Refers to the script `myscript` located within the `bin` directory inside your home directory.

Relative paths are often more convenient than absolute paths, especially when working with files and directories within your current working directory or its immediate vicinity. They also make your scripts more portable, as they don't rely on a fixed file system structure.

Understanding both absolute and relative paths is essential for navigating the Linux file system with confidence. As you become more comfortable with the command line, you'll instinctively choose the most appropriate type of path for each situation, making your journey through the file system smooth and efficient.

6. The Linux File System – A Hierarchical Wonderland

Imagine the Linux file system as a vast and intricate tree, with the root directory (/) as its trunk and directories branching out like limbs, each containing files and further subdirectories. This hierarchical structure provides a logical and organized way to store and access data, ensuring that every file and directory has a well-defined place within the system.

The Root Directory – Where It All Begins

The root directory, denoted by a single slash (/), is the starting point of the entire file system. It contains essential system files and directories, as well as mount points for other storage devices like hard drives and USB drives. As a regular user, you won't have write access to the root directory or most of its contents, as these are typically reserved for the system administrator to maintain system stability and security.

Common Directories and Their Purpose

Within the root directory, you'll find a variety of directories, each serving a specific purpose:

Directory	Description
/bin	Houses essential command binaries, the basic tools needed for the system to operate. Commands like **ls**, **pwd**, **clear**, and many others reside here.
/boot	Contains the Linux kernel and other files crucial for booting the system.
/dev	A special directory holding device files, representing physical and virtual devices like hard drives, terminals, and printers.
/etc	Stores system-wide configuration files that control the behavior of various programs and services.
/home	This directory is like a neighborhood, containing the home directories for each user on the system. Your home directory, denoted by the tilde symbol (~), is your personal space where you can create and store your files.
/lib	Houses shared library files used by the core system programs.
/media	The mount point for removable media such as USB drives and CD-ROMs.
/mnt	An older location used for manually mounting devices.
/opt	Often used for installing "optional" software packages.
/proc	A virtual file system providing information about running processes and system status.
/root	The home directory for the root user.
/sbin	Contains system administration commands, typically used by the superuser.
/tmp	A temporary storage area for files created by programs.
/usr	A large directory containing user applications, libraries, documentation, and other resources.
/var	Stores variable data such as log files, spool files, and temporary files created by various programs.

The Home Sweet Home Directory

As a regular user, your home directory will be your primary workspace. It's where you'll create and store your documents, downloads, music, pictures, and any other files you generate. You have full control over your home directory, allowing you to create, modify, and delete files and subdirectories as needed.

Understanding this hierarchical structure is crucial for navigating the Linux file system and organizing your data effectively. As you explore and work with different commands, you'll gain a deeper appreciation for the order and logic that this system provides.

7. Environment Variables – The System's Settings

Imagine a vast control panel with numerous knobs and switches that govern the behavior of a complex machine. **Environment variables** in Linux act as a similar control panel, storing values that influence how the system operates and how commands and programs behave. They are like global settings that convey information about the user, the system, and various configuration options.

PATH – The Command Locator

One of the most important environment variables is the PATH variable. It determines where the shell searches for executable programs when you type a command at the prompt.

To view the value of the PATH variable, use the echo command:

```
[noah@linux_lab ~]$ echo $PATH
/home/noah/bin:/usr/local/bin:/usr/bin:/bin
```

The output shows a colon-separated list of directories. When you type a command, the shell searches for it in each of these directories in the order they are listed. If the command is found in one of the directories, it is executed.

Other Important Variables

There are numerous other environment variables that influence various aspects of the system:

- USER: Stores the username of the current user.
- HOME: Specifies the path to the user's home directory.
- SHELL: Indicates the default shell used by the user.
- PWD: Contains the path to the current working directory.
- HOSTNAME: Stores the hostname of the machine.

You can view the values of these variables using the echo command, just like with the PATH variable:

```
[noah@linux_lab ~]$ echo $USER
noah
```

Environment Variables and Programs

Environment variables are not only used by the shell; they also influence the behavior of many programs and applications. For example, some programs use the `EDITOR` variable to determine the default text editor to use when editing files.

A Global Context

Environment variables provide a global context for your Linux system, influencing the behavior of commands, programs, and scripts. As you explore the command line and delve into shell scripting, you'll encounter various environment variables and learn how they shape the system's behavior.

8. Unix Philosophy and Legacy – A Glimpse into the Past

To truly grasp the essence of the Linux command line, it's essential to journey back in time and understand the philosophy and legacy that shaped its design. The roots of the Linux command line lie in the Unix operating system, a groundbreaking creation born in the late 1960s at Bell Labs.

The Unix Philosophy – Simplicity and Elegance

The creators of Unix, including Ken Thompson and Dennis Ritchie, were driven by a philosophy of simplicity and elegance. They believed in building small, modular tools that each performed a specific task well, rather than creating monolithic programs that tried to do everything. This philosophy led to the development of a vast collection of command line tools that could be combined in countless ways to achieve complex tasks.

Some key principles of the Unix philosophy include:
- **Do one thing and do it well**: Each program should focus on a specific task and excel at it.
- **Write programs that work together**: Programs should be designed to interact with each other seamlessly, allowing for easy integration and data exchange.
- **Handle text streams**: Text is a universal interface, making it easy for programs to communicate and process information.
- **Build for the user**: Programs should be user-friendly and provide clear and concise feedback.

"Everything is a File" – A Core Concept

One of the most fundamental concepts of Unix, and subsequently Linux, is the idea that "**everything is a file**". This means that devices, such as hard drives, printers, and terminals, are treated as files within the file system. This unified approach simplifies interaction with the system and allows for consistent treatment of data regardless of its source or destination.

The Legacy Continues – Linux and Beyond

Linux, inspired by Unix and its philosophy, inherited and expanded upon this rich legacy of command line tools. Today, the Linux command line offers a vast and powerful ecosystem of programs for virtually any task imaginable.

Understanding the history and philosophy behind the Unix/Linux command line provides insights into why it works the way it does. It helps explain the design decisions and conventions that have shaped the command line interface into the powerful and versatile tool it is today.

Chapter Summary

You've taken your first steps into the exciting world of the Linux command line. Let's recap the treasures you've discovered on this initial leg of our journey:

- We demystified the command line interface, revealing its power, flexibility, and efficiency.
- We explored terminal emulators, your gateway to accessing the shell and interacting with the command line.
- We deciphered the shell prompt, understanding its components and how it reflects your current location and user privileges.
- We mastered the basic commands `pwd`, `cd`, `ls`, and `clear`, giving you the tools to navigate the file system and reveal its contents.
- We explored the concepts of absolute and relative paths, understanding how they guide you through the hierarchical structure of the file system.
- We embarked on a tour of the Linux file system, discovering the root directory and various common directories and their purposes.
- We journeyed back in time to understand the Unix philosophy and legacy, appreciating the principles of simplicity, modularity, and text-based interaction that shaped the Linux command line.

Now that you're equipped with these foundational skills, it's time to practice and explore. Open your terminal emulator, experiment with the commands you've learned, and don't be afraid to venture into different directories and examine their contents. The Linux file system is your oyster, waiting to be discovered!

In the next chapter, we'll delve deeper into the art of file and directory manipulation, empowering you to become a true master of your digital domain.

Chapter 2:
File and Directory Wranglers

Files and directories are the building blocks of your digital world. They hold your documents, music, pictures, programs, and all the data that makes your computer tick. Mastering the art of **file and directory manipulation** is essential for navigating this world efficiently and keeping your data organized.

While graphical file managers offer a user-friendly way to interact with files and directories, the command line provides a more powerful and versatile toolkit. With command line tools, you can perform intricate file operations, automate tasks with scripts, and work with remote systems – capabilities that often lie beyond the reach of graphical interfaces.

In this chapter, we'll equip you with a set of essential commands for managing files and directories like a seasoned pro. You'll learn to create, copy, move, rename, and delete files and directories with precision and efficiency, all from the comfort of your terminal window.

1. mkdir – Building Your Digital Home

The first tool in our file management kit is the `mkdir` command, short for "make directory." As the name suggests, `mkdir` allows you to create new directories within the file system, providing a hierarchical structure for organizing your files. Think of it as building rooms and houses in your digital world, each with its own purpose and contents.

Creating Directories with Ease

Using `mkdir` is straightforward. Simply type `mkdir` followed by the name of the directory you want to create:

```
[noah@linux_lab ~]$ mkdir Music
```

This command creates a new directory named Music within your current working directory. You can verify its existence with `ls`:

```
[noah@linux_lab ~]$ ls
Music
```

Creating Parent Directories with -p

What if you want to create a directory within a directory that doesn't exist yet? For example, imagine you want to create a directory structure for your music collection, with separate directories for different artists and albums. You might want to create a directory for the band "Pink Floyd" within a directory named "Classic Rock", but the "Classic Rock" directory doesn't exist yet.

The `-p` option comes to the rescue! It instructs `mkdir` to create any necessary parent directories along the way.

```
[noah@linux_lab ~]$ mkdir -p Music/Classic\ Rock/Pink\ Floyd
```

This command creates the entire directory structure, including Music, Classic Rock, and Pink Floyd, even though they didn't exist before. The \ (backslash space) is used to escape the spaces in the directory names, ensuring that each directory name is treated as a single argument.

Building Multiple Directories

`mkdir` allows you to create multiple directories at once by specifying their names as separate arguments:

```
[noah@linux_lab ~]$ mkdir Documents Downloads Pictures
```

This command creates three directories – Documents, Downloads, and Pictures – all within your current working directory.

With `mkdir` in your command line toolkit, you have the power to build a well-structured and organized digital home for all your files and data.

2. touch – The Gentle File Creator

Sometimes, you need a file to exist, even if it's empty. Perhaps you're planning to add content later, or maybe the file's presence is required for a particular program or script. The `touch` command is your tool for creating empty files with a simple and elegant touch.

Creating Empty Files

To create an empty file, simply type `touch` followed by the desired filename:

```
[noah@linux_lab ~]$ touch notes.txt
```

This command creates an empty file named *notes.txt* in your current working directory. You can verify its existence with `ls`:

```
[noah@linux_lab ~]$ ls
notes.txt
```

Updating File Timestamps

`touch` has another superpower: it can update the timestamps associated with files. Every file in the Linux file system has three timestamps:
- **Access time**: The last time the file was read.
- **Modification time**: The last time the file's content was modified.

- **Change time**: The last time the file's metadata (e.g., permissions, ownership) was changed.

By default, `touch` updates both the access and modification times to the current time. This can be useful for marking a file as recently used or for affecting the behavior of programs that rely on file timestamps, such as backup scripts.

```
[noah@linux_lab ~]$ touch notes.txt
```

If you want to update only the access time or only the modification time, you can use the `-a` and `-m` options, respectively:

```
[noah@linux_lab ~]$ touch -a notes.txt  # Update only access time
[noah@linux_lab ~]$ touch -m notes.txt  # Update only modification time
```

The `touch` command is a versatile tool for creating empty files and manipulating timestamps, adding another layer of control and flexibility to your file management skills.

3. cp – The Master Duplicator

The `cp` command, short for "copy," is your tool for creating duplicates of files and directories. Whether you need to back up important data, share files with others, or simply create a working copy of a file, `cp` is your go-to command for duplication tasks.

Copying Files

To copy a single file, use the following syntax:

```
cp source_file destination_file
```

For example, to copy a file named song.ogg to a new file named backup.ogg, you would use:

```
[noah@linux_lab ~]$ cp song.ogg backup.ogg
```

This command creates an exact copy of song.ogg and names it backup.ogg in the same directory. If a file with the same name as the destination file already exists, `cp` will silently overwrite it.

Interactive Copying with -i

To prevent accidental overwrites, use the -i option, which prompts you for confirmation before overwriting an existing file:

```
[noah@linux_lab ~]$ cp -i song.ogg backup.ogg
cp: overwrite 'backup.ogg'?
```

Type y to confirm the overwrite, or any other key to cancel the operation.

Recursive Directory Copying with -r

To copy directories, you need the -r option, which stands for "recursive." This option tells cp to copy not only the directory itself but also all of its contents, including files and subdirectories:

```
[noah@linux_lab ~]$ cp -r Documents/ Projects/
```

This command creates a copy of the Documents directory and all its contents within the Projects directory.

Copying Multiple Files

You can copy multiple files at once by specifying them as a space-separated list, followed by the destination directory:

```
[noah@linux_lab ~]$ cp song1.ogg song2.ogg Music/
```

This command copies song1.ogg and song2.ogg into the Music directory.

The cp command is a powerful tool for creating duplicates of files and directories, offering options for safety, efficiency, and flexibility in your file management tasks.

4. mv – Moving and Renaming with Finesse

The mv command, short for "move," is a versatile tool for both relocating files and directories and giving them new names. It's like a skilled choreographer, gracefully moving your files and directories to their designated positions on the file system stage and giving them new identities when needed.

Moving Files and Directories

To move a file or directory, use the following syntax:

```
mv source_file destination_file
```

For example, to move a file named report.txt from your home directory to the Documents directory, you would use:

```
[noah@linux_lab ~]$ mv report.txt Documents/
```

This command relocates report.txt to the Documents directory, leaving no trace of it in its original location.

You can also move multiple files at once by specifying them as a space-separated list, followed by the destination directory:

```
[noah@linux_lab ~]$ mv image1.jpg image2.jpg Pictures/
```

This command moves image1.jpg and image2.jpg into the Pictures directory.

Renaming Files and Directories

mv doubles as a renaming tool. When you specify a new name for a file or directory as the destination, mv renames it while keeping it in the same location:

```
[noah@linux_lab ~]$ mv notes.txt ideas.txt
```

This command changes the name of the file from notes.txt to ideas.txt within your home directory.

The Destination Determines the Action

The behavior of mv depends on the nature of the destination:
- **If the destination is an existing directory**: The source file or directory is moved into the destination directory.
- **If the destination is a non-existent filename**: The source file or directory is renamed to the specified filename.
- **If the destination is an existing file**: The source file will overwrite the destination file (with a prompt if the -i option is used).

As with cp, the -i option prompts you for confirmation before overwriting existing files, providing an extra layer of safety.

The mv command, with its dual ability to move and rename, is an invaluable asset in your command line toolbox, allowing you to orchestrate the organization of your files and directories with elegance and precision.

5. rm – The Careful Destroyer

With great power comes great responsibility, and the rm command, short for "remove," is a powerful tool that demands respect and caution. rm allows you to delete files and directories, but unlike the Recycle Bin you might be familiar with in other operating systems, there's no undo button in the command line world. Once you delete something with rm, it's gone for good.

Removing Files

To delete a single file, use the following syntax:

```
rm filename
```

For example, to remove a file named temp.txt, you would use:

```
[noah@linux_lab ~]$ rm temp.txt
```

The file is silently deleted, without any confirmation or warning.

Interactive Deletion with -i

To avoid accidental deletion, use the -i option, which prompts you for confirmation before removing each file:

```
[noah@linux_lab ~]$ rm -i important.txt
rm: remove regular empty file 'important.txt'?
```

Type y to confirm the deletion, or any other key to keep the file safe and sound.

Recursive Directory Removal with -r

To delete directories, you need the `-r` option, which stands for "recursive." This option tells `rm` to delete not only the directory itself but also all of its contents, including files and subdirectories:

```
[noah@linux_lab ~]$ rm -r Old\ Projects/
```

This command recursively deletes the Old Projects directory and everything within it.

The Permanence of Deletion

It's crucial to emphasize the **irreversible nature** of `rm`. Once you delete a file or directory with `rm`, it's gone from your system and extremely difficult, if not impossible, to recover. Therefore, it's essential to exercise caution and double-check your commands before pressing Enter.

Safe Practices and Potential Pitfalls

Here are some tips to ensure you wield the power of `rm` responsibly:
- **Always double-check your commands before pressing Enter**. A typo could lead to the deletion of unintended files.
- **Use the `-i` option for interactive deletion**, especially when working with important files or directories.
- **Be extremely cautious with wildcards**. A misplaced space or an overly broad pattern could lead to the deletion of more files than intended. For example, `rm * .txt` would delete all files in the current directory, followed by an error message about a non-existent file named .txt.
- **Consider using a version control system** like Git to track changes and provide a safety net in case of accidental deletions.

By understanding the power and permanence of `rm` and adhering to safe practices, you can confidently use this command to remove unwanted files and directories while keeping your valuable data protected.

6. Wildcards – Unleashing the Power of Patterns

Imagine you're a librarian tasked with finding all the books on a specific topic, say, "Linux system administration." You wouldn't want to search for each book title individually; instead, you'd look for a pattern, perhaps books with titles containing the words "Linux" and "administration." Wildcards in the command line world are like these patterns, allowing you to select files and directories based on character combinations, making your tasks more efficient and powerful.

Wildcard Characters - Your Pattern Matching Arsenal

The shell provides three main wildcard characters:

Wildcard	Description
* (asterisk)	Matches any sequence of characters, including no characters. For example, *.txt would match all files with the .txt extension, and **Documents/*** would match all files and directories within the Documents directory.
? (question mark)	Matches any single character. For example, **Data????.csv** would match files beginning with "Data" followed by exactly four characters and ending with the **.csv** extension.
[ ] (square brackets)	Matches any single character within the brackets. For example, **[abc]*** would match files starting with "a", "b", or "c", and **BACKUP.[0-9][0-9][0-9]** would match files beginning with "BACKUP." followed by exactly three numerals.

Building Complex Selection Patterns

You can combine these wildcards to create intricate selection criteria. Here are a few examples:

- ***[[:lower:]]**: Matches all files ending with a lowercase letter.
- **[![:digit:]]***: Matches all files that do not start with a number.
- **[A-Z]*[0-9][0-9]**: Matches all files starting with an uppercase letter and ending with two digits.

Wildcards in Action

Wildcards can be used with any command that accepts filenames as arguments. Here are a few examples:

- `ls *.jpg`: Lists all files with the .jpg extension in the current directory.
- `cp *.pdf Documents/`: Copies all PDF files to the Documents directory.
- `rm -i *.bak`: Interactively deletes all files with the .bak extension.

Wildcard Wielding with Caution

While wildcards are incredibly powerful, they require careful handling:

- **Always double-check your wildcard patterns before using them with commands like** rm. An overly broad pattern could lead to the unintended deletion of files.
- **Test your wildcards with** ls **before using them with other commands.** This allows you to see exactly which files will be affected.
- **Use the -i (interactive) option with commands like** rm when using wildcards to ensure you have a chance to confirm each deletion.

By understanding the power and potential pitfalls of wildcards, you can leverage them effectively to perform efficient and sophisticated file management tasks.

7. File Attributes – Decoding the Secrets of ls -l

The ls -l command, as we encountered in Chapter 1, provides a detailed listing of files and directories, revealing their attributes and characteristics. It's like having an X-ray vision into the file system, allowing you to see beyond filenames and understand the inner workings of each file and directory.

The Long Listing Format

When you execute ls -l, you'll see a table-like output with each row representing a file or directory and each column providing specific information about its attributes. Let's dissect the meaning of each field:

Field	Description
File Type	The very first character in each row indicates the file type: • - : A regular file, containing data such as text, images, or program code. • d : A directory, holding other files and directories. • l : A symbolic link, pointing to another file or directory.
Permissions	The next nine characters represent the file's permissions for the owner, group, and others. Each set of three characters indicates read (r), write (w), and execute (x) permissions. A hyphen (-) in place of a permission letter means that permission is not granted.
Link Count	This number indicates the number of hard links associated with the file. We'll explore hard links in the next chapter.
Owner	The username of the user who owns the file.

Group	The name of the group that owns the file.
File Size	The size of the file in bytes.
Modification Date and Time	The date and time the file was last modified.
Filename	The name of the file or directory.

Understanding File Types

The file type field tells you the basic nature of the file:
- **Regular files**: These are the most common type of files, containing data that programs and users interact with.
- **Directories**: Directories act as containers for other files and directories, providing a hierarchical organization for the file system.
- **Symbolic links**: These are special files that point to other files or directories. We'll explore symbolic links and their uses in the next chapter.

Introduction to File Permissions

File permissions determine who can access a file and what actions they can perform. The three sets of permissions (read, write, execute) apply to three categories of users:
- **Owner**: The user who owns the file.
- **Group**: The group that owns the file.
- **Others**: All other users on the system.

Here's a breakdown of each permission:
- **Read (r)**: Allows viewing the contents of a file or listing the contents of a directory.
- **Write (w)**: Allows modifying the contents of a file or creating, deleting, and renaming files within a directory.
- **Execute (x)**: Allows executing a file as a program or entering a directory with cd.

We'll delve deeper into file permissions and their management in later chapters.

A Glimpse into Ownership

Every file and directory is owned by a specific user and group. The owner has primary control over the file's permissions and actions, while the group owner-ship allows for shared access among a group of users.

Understanding file attributes through ls -l is a crucial step towards mastering file management in Linux. By decoding the information presented in the long listing, you gain insights into the properties and access control of your files and directories, empowering you to manage them effectively and securely.

Chapter Summary

In this chapter, you've transformed into a skilled file and directory wrangler, wielding a powerful set of command line tools to manage your digital domain:

- We explored the fundamental commands for file and directory manipulation: `mkdir` for creating directories, `touch` for creating empty files and updating timestamps, `cp` for duplicating files and directories, `mv` for moving and renaming, and the mighty `rm` for careful deletion.
- We unlocked the power of wildcards, learning how to use patterns to select multiple files and directories efficiently.
- We deciphered the secrets of file attributes, understanding the meaning behind each field in the `ls -l` output and gaining insights into file types, permissions, and ownership.

Remember, with great power comes great responsibility, especially when it comes to deleting files with `rm`. Always double-check your commands and use the `-i` option for interactive deletion to prevent accidental data loss.

As you continue your command line journey, you'll find these file management skills invaluable for organizing your data, working with programs and scripts, and collaborating with others.

In the next chapter, we'll explore the fascinating world of linking, discovering how to create multiple names for files and directories and unlock new levels of file management mastery.

Chapter 3:
Linking Masterclass

In this chapter, we'll embark on a masterclass of linking, unraveling the mysteries of hard links and symbolic links. You'll learn how to forge these connections using the `ln` command, explore their practical applications, and navigate potential pitfalls with caution and expertise. So, prepare to become a linking virtuoso as we delve into this fascinating aspect of the Linux file system!

1. Linking – Creating Connections in the File System

Imagine you have a prized possession, say, a rare and valuable book. You want to keep it safe and secure in your personal library, but you also want to share it with friends and colleagues who might appreciate its content. In the physical world, this presents a dilemma – you can't have the book in two places at once. However, in the digital realm of the Linux file system, **linking** offers a clever solution.

Linking allows you to create multiple names, or aliases, for a single file or directory. It's like having multiple entry points to the same location in the file system, each leading to the same underlying data. This ability to create connections between files and directories opens up a world of possibilities for file organization, sharing, and efficient data management.

Why Use Links?

Linking offers several advantages:
- **File Sharing**: You can share files and directories with other users without creating duplicate copies, saving valuable disk space and ensuring everyone is working with the same version of the data.
- **Organization and Efficiency**: Links provide a way to organize files and directories logically, regardless of their physical location on the disk. You can create shortcuts to frequently accessed files or group related files together using links, even if they reside in different directories.
- **Multiple Versions and Backups**: Links can help manage multiple versions of a file or maintain backups without consuming excessive storage space.

Types of Links

There are two primary types of links in the Linux file system:
- **Hard links**: These links are like creating multiple name tags for the same physical book. They all refer to the same underlying data blocks on the disk, and deleting one hard link doesn't affect the others or the original file.
- **Symbolic links (symlinks)**: These links are like creating a pointer or shortcut to the book's location in the library. They don't directly reference the data blocks; instead, they contain a path to the target file or directory.

We'll explore both types of links in detail, understanding their differences and learning how to create and use them effectively.

2. Hard Links – Inode Allies

Imagine you have a physical book with multiple identical copies of the cover attached to it. Each cover represents a different name for the same book, allowing you to access its content from various places in your library. Hard links in the Linux file system operate in a similar way, creating multiple directory entries, or hard links, that all point to the same underlying data blocks on the disk.

Understanding Inodes

To grasp the concept of hard links, we need to delve a little deeper into the structure of the file system. Each file is associated with an **inode**, a data structure that stores information about the file, such as its size, permissions, ownership, and the location of its data blocks on the disk.

When you create a hard link, you're essentially creating a new directory entry that points to the same inode as the original file. This means that both the original file and the hard link share the same inode and, consequently, the same data blocks.

Creating Hard Links with ln

To forge a hard link, we use the ln command:

```
ln target_file link_name
```

For example, to create a hard link named *favorites.txt* for a file called *playlist.txt*, you would use:

```
[noah@linux_lab ~]$ ln playlist.txt favorites.txt
```

Now, both *playlist.txt* and *favorites.txt* refer to the same file on the disk. You can modify the contents of either file, and the changes will be reflected in both, as they share the same underlying data.

The Link Count – A Tale of Shared Inodes

When you use ls -l to view the long listing of a file with hard links, you'll notice the link count field. This number indicates how many hard links point to the same inode. For example:

```
[noah@linux_lab ~]$ ls -l playlist.txt favorites.txt
-rw-rw-r-- 2 noah noah 765 Oct 26 14:02 favorites.txt
-rw-rw-r-- 2 noah noah 765 Oct 26 14:02 playlist.txt
```

We can see that both files have a link count of 2, indicating that two hard links point to the same inode (and therefore the same data).

Limitations of Hard Links

Hard links, while useful, have limitations:
- **Same File System**: You cannot create a hard link to a file on a different file system (e.g., a different disk partition). Hard links only work within the same file system.
- **No Directories**: Hard links cannot be created for directories (with the exception of the special . and .. directories). This is to prevent circular references and potential problems with file system traversal.

Despite these limitations, hard links remain a valuable tool for creating multiple access points to files, particularly within the same file system.

3. Symbolic Links – The Flexible Pathfinders

While hard links are like multiple entryways to the same room, symbolic links, also known as symlinks, are like signposts pointing the way to a different location. A symbolic link is a special type of file that contains a reference, or path, to another file or directory. It acts as a pointer, redirecting any access to the link to its target.

The Magic of File Pointers

Imagine you have a note on your desk that says, "The book you're looking for is on the second shelf, third from the left." This note is like a symbolic link – it doesn't contain the actual book, but it provides directions to its location. Symbolic links in the Linux file system operate in a similar fashion, storing the path to the target file or directory.

Creating Symbolic Links with ln -s

To create a symbolic link, we use the ln command with the -s option:

```
ln -s target_file link_name
```

For example, to create a symbolic link named recent_notes that points to a file called */home/noah/Documents/notes.txt*, you would use:

```
[noah@linux_lab ~]$ ln -s /home/noah/Documents/notes.txt recent_notes
```

Now, accessing recent_notes is like accessing the actual file */home/noah/Documents/notes.txt*. Any changes made to recent_notes will affect the target file, and vice versa.

Links and Targets – A Delicate Dance

It's important to understand the distinction between a symbolic link and its target:
- **The symbolic link itself is a separate file** with its own inode and file attributes.
- **The link contains the path to the target file or directory.**
- **Deleting the symbolic link does not affect the target file or directory.**
- **If the target file is deleted or moved, the symbolic link becomes broken**, as it now points to a non-existent location.

Flexibility of Symbolic Links

Symbolic links offer greater flexibility than hard links:
- **Across File Systems**: Symlinks can point to files or directories on different file systems, even on different physical devices.
- **Linking to Directories**: Symlinks can be created for directories, allowing for convenient shortcuts and organization.

This flexibility makes symbolic links a powerful tool for managing files and directories in a variety of situations.

4. Linking in Action – Practical Applications

Now that we've grasped the concepts of hard links and symbolic links, let's explore how these versatile tools can be applied in real-world scenarios to enhance file management and system organization.

File Sharing – Collaboration without Duplication

Imagine you and a colleague are working on a project together, and you need to share a set of documents and resources. Instead of creating duplicate copies of the files, which could lead to version conflicts and wasted disk space, you can use symbolic links to create a shared project directory:

1. Create a project directory:

```
[noah@linux_lab ~]$ mkdir ProjectX
```

2. Move the project files into the directory:

```
[noah@linux_lab ~]$ mv document1.txt document2.odt images/ ProjectX/
```

3. Create symbolic links in your colleague's home directory:

```
[noah@linux_lab ~]$ ln -s /home/noah/ProjectX/ /home/colleague/ProjectX
```

Now, both you and your colleague have access to the same set of project files through the *ProjectX* directory in your respective home directories, fostering collaboration without unnecessary duplication.

Shortcuts – Instant Access to Frequently Used Files

Do you have files or directories that you access frequently, buried deep within the file system? Symbolic links can create convenient shortcuts, allowing you to access them quickly and easily from any location:

```
[noah@linux_lab ~]$ ln -s /usr/share/backgrounds/my_favorite_wallpaper.jpg
wallpaper
```

This command creates a symlink named wallpaper in your home directory that points to your favorite wallpaper image. Now, you can quickly change your desktop background by referencing the wallpaper link, without having to type the full path each time.

Version Control – Managing the Evolution of Files

Links can be a valuable tool for maintaining multiple versions of a file:

```
[noah@linux_lab ~]$ cp presentation.odp presentation_v1.odp
[noah@linux_lab ~]$ ln -s presentation.odp presentation_latest.odp
```

In this example, we create a copy of the original presentation and then create a symlink named presentation_latest.odp that points to the current version. As you make changes and create new versions, you simply update the symlink to point to the latest file, keeping your workflow organized and ensuring you're always working with the most up-to-date version.

File Organization – Grouping by Logic, not Location

Links allow you to group related files together, even if they reside in different directories:

```
[noah@linux_lab ~]$ mkdir -p Work/Projects/ProjectA Work/Projects/ProjectB
[noah@linux_lab ~]$ ln -s Work/Projects/ProjectA/report.pdf Work/Reports/
[noah@linux_lab ~]$ ln -s Work/Projects/ProjectB/data.csv Work/Data/
```

This example demonstrates creating a logical organization for project files and reports using symlinks, providing a structured and efficient way to access related information.

These are just a few examples of the many ways linking can enhance your file management skills. As you explore and experiment, you'll discover new and creative ways to use links to optimize your workflow and organize your digital world.

5. Linking with Care – Potential Pitfalls

While linking offers numerous advantages, it's important to be aware of potential pitfalls and exercise caution, especially when working with system files or directories.

Broken Links – The Dangling Pointers

A symbolic link becomes broken if its target file or directory is deleted or moved. When you attempt to access a broken link, you'll encounter an error message indicating that the target cannot be found.

```
[noah@linux_lab ~]$ ls -l broken_link
lrwxrwxrwx 1 noah noah 15 Oct 27 10:32 broken_link -> /home/noah/missing_file.txt
```

```
[noah@linux_lab ~]$ cat broken_link
cat: broken_link: No such file or directory
```

In this example, the symlink broken_link points to a file that no longer exists, rendering the link useless.

To avoid broken links, be mindful of the relationships between links and their targets, and ensure that you don't inadvertently delete or move target files that are referenced by existing links.

Circular Links – The Infinite Loop

A **circular link** occurs when a symbolic link creates a loop, pointing back to itself or to another link that ultimately leads back to the original link. This can create an infinite loop when programs or commands attempt to traverse the linked files, potentially leading to system instability or crashes.

For example, avoid creating a link like this:

```
[noah@linux_lab ~]$ ln -s link1 link2
[noah@linux_lab ~]$ ln -s link2 link1
```

These commands create a circular reference, where link1 points to link2, which in turn points back to link1, creating a never-ending loop.

Caution with System Files

While it's generally safe to use links within your home directory or for personal projects, be cautious when working with system files or directories. Incorrectly creating or modifying links for critical system files can lead to system malfunction or even prevent your system from booting properly.

Always back up important files before making changes, and exercise caution when using links in system areas.

By understanding these potential pitfalls and using links judiciously, you can harness their power while keeping your file system organized and secure.

Chapter Summary

Congratulations, you've now mastered the art of linking, adding another valuable skill to your command line repertoire. Let's review the key takeaways from this chapter:

- We explored the concept of linking and its benefits for file sharing, organization, efficiency, and version control.
- We learned how to create both hard links and symbolic links using the `ln` command, understanding the differences between these two types of links and their respective strengths and limitations.
- We delved into practical applications of linking, such as sharing project files, creating shortcuts, managing file versions, and organizing data logically.
- We discussed the potential pitfalls of using links, including broken links and circular references, emphasizing the importance of caution and careful planning.

Linking is a powerful tool, but like any powerful tool, it requires respect and understanding. By using links thoughtfully and with awareness of their potential pitfalls, you can create a more organized, efficient, and collaborative digital environment.

Chapter 4:
Command Anatomy and
Discovery

This chapter will equip you with the knowledge and tools to dissect commands and unlock their secrets. You'll learn to differentiate between different types of commands, discover methods for identifying their locations within the file system, and explore various ways to access their documentation and usage information. With these skills in hand, you'll be well on your way to mastering the command line and becoming a true command line wizard!

1. Dissecting Commands – Understanding the Building Blocks

Every command you encounter on the Linux command line follows a basic structure, composed of three main elements:

```
command_name [options] [arguments]
```

Let's examine each component:

component	Description
command_name	This is the name of the command you want to execute, such as **ls**, **cd**, **cp**, or **mkdir**. The command name tells the shell which program or built-in function to run.
[options]	Options, also known as flags, are modifiers that affect the behavior of the command. They are typically preceded by a hyphen (-) and consist of a single letter or a longer descriptive word (preceded by two hyphens --). For example, the -l option for **ls** instructs it to display the long listing format, and the **--help** option for many commands displays a help message.
[arguments]	Arguments are the input data upon which the command operates. This could be filenames, directory names, usernames, or any other type of data that the command requires to perform its task. For example, in the command **cp file1.txt file2.txt**, *file1.txt* and *file2.txt* are arguments representing the source and destination files for the copy operation.

Options – Modifying Command Behavior

Options provide a way to customize the way a command works, offering a wide range of possibilities depending on the specific command. Here are a few common types of options:

- **Action options**: These options specify the action a command should perform. For example, the -r option for rm instructs it to recursively delete directories.
- **Selection options**: These options control which items the command operates on. For example, the -a option for ls tells it to list all files, including hidden files.

- **Output format options**: These options modify the way the command displays its output. For example, the -h option for ls displays file sizes in a human-readable format.

Short Options vs. Long Options

Many commands offer both short and long options. Short options consist of a single letter preceded by a hyphen, while long options use a descriptive word preceded by two hyphens. For example, the -a and --all options for ls are equivalent, both instructing it to list all files.

Short options are often preferred for brevity when typing commands on the command line, while long options can improve readability, especially in scripts and documentation.

By understanding the structure of commands and the role of options and arguments, you gain a deeper appreciation for the flexibility and power of the command line.

2. Command Types – A Diverse Ecosystem

The Linux command line is teeming with a diverse array of commands, each playing a unique role in this digital ecosystem. These commands can be categorized into four main types:

Command Type	Description
Executable Programs	These are files containing compiled code or scripts that the shell can directly execute. They reside in directories listed within your PATH environment variable, such as /**bin**, /**usr**/**bin**, and ~/**bin**. Executable programs form the majority of commands you'll encounter, providing a wide range of functionality. • **Compiled Programs**: These programs are written in languages like C or C++ and compiled into machine code that the computer's processor can directly understand. They tend to be highly efficient and optimized for performance. For example, the **ls** command, which lists directory contents, is a compiled program located in the /**bin** directory. • **Scripts**: These are programs written in scripting languages such as Bash, Python, Perl, or Ruby. Scripts are interpreted line by line, making them easier to write and modify compared to compiled programs. For instance, you might write a Bash script to automate a series of file management tasks or a Python script to analyze data.
Shell Builtins	These are commands that are built into the shell itself. They provide core functionality for interacting with the shell and managing basic tasks. Examples of shell builtins include **cd** (change directory), **echo** (display text), **pwd** (print working directory), **exit** (terminate the shell session), and **history** (view command history). These commands are always available within the shell, regardless of your current directory or the contents of your PATH variable.
Aliases	Aliases are user-defined shortcuts for commands. They allow you to create your own custom commands by assigning a new name to an existing command or a sequence of commands. For example, you might create an alias **ll** that executes **ls -l**, providing a quicker way to view the long listing format. Aliases are defined in your shell configuration files, such as ~/**.bashrc**, and can be used to simplify frequently used commands or personalize your command line experience.
Functions	Shell functions are like mini-scripts that can be defined within your shell environment or in scripts. They provide a way to encapsulate a series of commands and execute them as a single unit, often with arguments and local variables. Functions can improve the modularity and organization of your scripts and enhance code reusability.

Understanding the different types of commands and their characteristics is essential for navigating the command line effectively. In the following sections, we'll explore tools that help you identify the type and location of commands, as well as access their documentation and usage information.

3. type – Revealing a Command's Identity

As you encounter various commands, you might wonder about their true nature – are they executable programs, shell builtins, or perhaps aliases in disguise? The `type` command acts as a detective, revealing the identity of a command and how the shell interprets it.

Unveiling the Command's True Form

Using `type` is straightforward. Simply type `type` followed by the name of the command you want to investigate:

```
[noah@linux_lab ~]$ type ls
ls is aliased to `ls --color=auto'
```

In this example, `type` reveals that `ls` is not a simple executable program; it's actually an alias configured to execute `ls --color=auto`, which explains why the output of `ls` is displayed in color.

Let's try `type` with a few other commands:

```
[noah@linux_lab ~]$ type cd
cd is a shell builtin
[noah@linux_lab ~]$ type cp
cp is /bin/cp
```

Here, we discover that `cd` is a shell builtin, a command built into the Bash shell itself, while `cp` is an executable program located in the `/bin` directory.

A Handy Tool for Understanding

The `type` command is a valuable tool for understanding the behavior of commands and troubleshooting issues. It allows you to:

- **Identify the type of a command**: Determine whether it's an executable program, a shell builtin, an alias, or a function.
- **Uncover aliases**: See the underlying commands hidden behind aliases.
- **Locate executable programs**: Discover the directory where an executable program resides.

By using `type`, you can gain a clearer understanding of the commands you use and how the shell interprets your instructions.

4. which – Locating Executable Commands

While `type` reveals the nature of a command, the `which` command acts as a GPS, pinpointing the exact location of executable programs within the file system. This is particularly useful when you have multiple versions of a program installed or when you need to know the full path of a command for scripting purposes.

Finding the Command's Home

To use `which`, simply type it followed by the name of the command you want to locate:

```
[noah@linux_lab ~]$ which python3
/usr/bin/python3
```

In this example, which reveals that the python3 command resides in the **/usr/bin** directory. This is the full path to the executable program that the shell runs when you type python3 at the prompt.

which and the PATH

The `which` command works by searching the directories listed in your PATH environment variable. Remember, the PATH variable contains a colon-separated list of directories where the shell looks for executable programs.

```
[noah@linux_lab ~]$ echo $PATH
/home/noah/bin:/usr/local/bin:/usr/bin:/bin
```

If a command is not found in any of these directories, `which` will return nothing.

Limitations of which

It's important to remember that `which` only works for executable programs, not for shell builtins or aliases:

```
[noah@linux_lab ~]$ which cd
[noah@linux_lab ~]$
```

Since `cd` is a shell builtin, `which` doesn't find it in the PATH.

By using `which` alongside `type`, you can gain a comprehensive understanding of a command's identity and location within the file system.

5. man – The Manual at Your Fingertips

Imagine having a comprehensive encyclopedia of command knowledge readily available at your fingertips. The `man` command, short for "manual," is just that – a gateway to a vast collection of documentation for the numerous commands available on your Linux system.

Accessing the Treasure Trove of Knowledge

To access the manual page for a specific command, simply type `man` followed by the command name:

```
[noah@linux_lab ~]$ man ls
```

This will open the manual page for the `ls` command in a pager program like `less`, allowing you to scroll through the documentation and search for specific information.

Navigating the Manual Page

Manual pages follow a common structure, typically containing the following sections:

Section	Description
NAME	The name of the command and a brief description of its purpose.

SYNOPSIS	A summary of the command's syntax, including options and arguments.
DESCRIPTION	A detailed explanation of the command's functionality and behavior.
OPTIONS	A list of the available options, their meanings, and their effects on the command's behavior.
EXAMPLES	Illustrative examples of how to use the command in various situations.
SEE ALSO	References to related commands or documentation.

While viewing a man page, you can use the following keys to navigate:
- **Up/Down arrows or j/k**: Scroll through the page line by line.
- **Page Up/Page Down or b/Space**: Scroll up or down one page at a time.
- **/search_term**: Search for a specific word or phrase within the page.
- **n/N**: Jump to the next or previous match of your search.
- **q**: Quit the man page and return to the shell prompt.

Exploring Different Sections

The manual is organized into sections, each covering a different category of commands:
- 1: User Commands (most common)
- 2: System Calls
- 3: Library Functions
- 4: Special Files (devices)
- 5: File Formats and Conventions
- 6: Games and Amusements
- 7: Miscellaneous
- 8: System Administration Commands

To access a specific section of the manual, add the section number before the command name:

```
[noah@linux_lab ~]$ man 5 passwd
```

This command displays the manual page for the `passwd` file format, which resides in section 5 of the manual.

The `man` command is an invaluable resource for any command line user, providing a wealth of information about the tools at your disposal. As you encounter new commands or need to refresh your memory on existing ones, `man` is always there to guide you.

6. info – The GNU Documentation System

While `man` pages provide a concise reference for commands, the GNU Project offers a more extensive documentation system known as `info`. Info pages are like interactive hypertext documents, providing in-depth information, tutorials, and examples for GNU programs and utilities.

Entering the World of Info

To access the info page for a program, simply type `info` followed by the program name:

```
[noah@linux_lab ~]$ info coreutils
```

This command launches the `info` reader and displays the main info page for the `coreutils` package, which contains many essential command line utilities like `ls`, `cp`, `mv`, and `rm`.

Navigating the Info Labyrinth

Info pages are organized into nodes, each containing a specific topic or section of information. Nodes are linked together, allowing you to navigate through the documentation in a non-linear fashion, much like browsing a website.

Here are some key commands for navigating info pages:

- **Up/Down arrows or Previous/Next line**: Scroll up or down one line at a time.
- **Page Up/Page Down or Previous/Next page**: Move to the previous or next page within the current node.
- **n/p**: Jump to the next or previous node in the sequence.
- **u**: Move up one level in the node hierarchy (often to a menu or index).
- **l**: Go back to the last visited node.
- **mMenu**: Jump to a specific menu or node by typing its name.
- **Enter**: Follow a link to another node. Links are displayed with an asterisk (*) before the text.
- **q**: Quit the info reader and return to the shell prompt.

A Deeper Dive into Documentation

Info pages offer several advantages over man pages:

- **More comprehensive**: Info pages often contain more detailed explanations, examples, and tutorials than man pages.
- **Hyperlinked structure**: The linked nature of info pages allows for non-linear exploration and easy access to related information.
- **Searchable**: You can search for specific words or phrases within info pages using the / command, similar to searching in `less` or `vim`.

While info pages might seem daunting at first, their in-depth coverage and hyperlinked structure make them a valuable resource for gaining a deeper understanding of GNU programs and utilities. As you become more familiar with the info system, you'll appreciate its ability to provide comprehensive and easily accessible documentation.

7. apropos and whatis – Searching for Clues

Sometimes, you have a vague idea of what you want to accomplish but don't know the exact command or tool to use. The `apropos` and `whatis` commands act as your investigative partners, helping you search the vast landscape of commands and manual pages for potential matches.

apropos – Finding Commands by Keyword

The `apropos` command searches the descriptions of man pages for keywords and displays a list of matching results. It's like having a librarian who can quickly scan through all the book summaries and point you to the ones that might be relevant to your topic.

For example, if you're looking for commands related to networking, you could use:

```
[noah@linux_lab ~]$ apropos network
hostname (1)              - show or set the system's host name
netstat (8)               - Print network connections, routing tables...
ip (8)                    - show / manipulate routing, devices, policy...
ping (8)                  - send ICMP ECHO_REQUEST to network hosts
traceroute (8)            - print the route packets trace to network host
```

The output of `apropos` displays the command name, followed by the section number of the manual page and a brief description.

whatis – A Quick Glimpse

The whatis command provides a concise, one-line summary of a man page. It's like a quick glance at the back cover of a book, giving you a brief synopsis of its contents.

```
[noah@linux_lab ~]$ whatis man
man (1)                - an interface to the on-line reference manuals
man (7)                - macros to format man pages
```

This command tells you that the man command itself is documented in section 1 of the manual and is used to access the online reference manuals (i.e., man pages).

Searching with Precision

Both apropos and whatis use the same database of man page descriptions, so they often produce similar results. However, apropos tends to be more comprehensive, displaying a list of potential matches, while whatis provides a more focused, single-line summary.

Use apropos when you're exploring a broader topic or searching for commands related to a general concept, and use whatis when you need a quick reminder of a specific command's purpose.

8. The Importance of Seeking Help

As you venture further into the command line wilderness, you'll inevitably encounter unfamiliar commands, perplexing options, or unexpected results. Don't despair, brave adventurer! Seeking help is not a sign of weakness; it's a mark of a wise and resourceful explorer.

The Linux world is brimming with helpful resources and communities eager to assist you on your journey:

- **Manual Pages and Info Pages**: As we've seen, the man and info commands are your built-in guides, providing detailed documentation and usage information for countless commands and programs.
- **Online Resources**: The internet is a treasure trove of tutorials, forums, and communities dedicated to Linux and the command line. Websites like Stack Overflow, Ask Ubuntu, and LinuxQuestions.org offer a wealth of knowledge and support from fellow users and experts.
- **Distribution Documentation**: Many Linux distributions provide extensive documentation, including user guides, wikis, and forums specific to their distribution.

- **Community Support**: Local Linux user groups and online communities offer a chance to connect with other enthusiasts, ask questions, and learn from each other's experiences.

Chapter Summary

In this chapter, we've dissected the anatomy of commands, uncovering the secrets of their structure and the diverse ecosystem of command types within the Linux world:

- We learned to identify the building blocks of commands: command names, options, and arguments, and explored how options modify command behavior.
- We distinguished between executable programs, shell builtins, aliases, and functions, understanding the unique roles each type plays in the command line environment.
- We explored the `type` and `which` commands, which act as detectives, revealing a command's identity and location within the file system.
- We unlocked the treasure troves of knowledge contained within `man` pages and `info` documents, learning how to access and navigate these valuable resources to find detailed information about commands and programs.
- We discovered the power of `apropos` and `whatis` for searching command references and finding the right tools for the job.
- We emphasized the importance of seeking help and utilizing the vast array of resources available to Linux users.

Remember, understanding the behavior of commands is essential for using the command line effectively. By utilizing the tools and resources we've covered in this chapter, you can become a more informed and confident command line explorer. As you continue your journey, you'll find that the ability to dissect commands and access their documentation will be invaluable for expanding your knowledge and mastering the art of the Linux command line.

Chapter 5:
Taming the Output

We'll explore the concept of standard streams – the conduits through which data flows between commands, files, and the user. You'll become a master plumber, wielding redirection operators to channel the output of your commands into files, combine streams, or even discard unwanted information. So, grab your metaphorical wrench and prepare to master the art of redirection!

1. Standard Streams – The Flow of Information

Imagine a bustling city with a network of pipes carrying water, sewage, and other essential resources. Similarly, the Linux command line has a system of **standard streams** that facilitate the flow of information between commands, files, and the user. These streams act as conduits for input and output, allowing programs to communicate and exchange data.

The Three Musketeers of Streams

There are three primary standard streams:
- **Standard Input (stdin)**: This stream is the default source of input for commands. By default, it's connected to the keyboard, allowing you to type input that programs can read and process.
- **Standard Output (stdout)**: This stream is the default destination for a command's normal output, which typically includes the results of its operation or any generated data. By default, standard output is directed to the terminal screen, displaying the command's results for you to see.
- **Standard Error (stderr)**: This stream is used for displaying error messages and diagnostic information. Like standard output, it's directed to the terminal screen by default, ensuring that error messages are visible even if the standard output is redirected.

Commands and Their Streams

Most commands interact with these standard streams in the following ways:
- **Reading from stdin**: Commands like `cat`, `sort`, `grep`, and many others can accept input from standard input if no filename arguments are provided. This allows you to pipe the output of one command into another, creating powerful data processing pipelines.
- **Writing to stdout**: Most commands send their normal output to standard output, displaying the results on the terminal screen.
- **Writing to stderr**: When a command encounters an error or needs to display diagnostic information, it sends messages to standard error, ensuring that these messages are visible even if the standard output is redirected.

Understanding the role and behavior of these standard streams is crucial for working with the command line effectively. In the next section, we'll explore how to control the flow of information using **redirection**, allowing you to change the source and destination of these streams and harness their power for a variety of tasks.

2. Redirection – Changing the Course of the Stream

Imagine a river flowing downstream, following its natural course. With dams, canals, and other engineering feats, we can redirect the flow of water, channeling it to where it's needed most. Similarly, **redirection** in the Linux command line allows you to alter the default flow of information, directing input and output streams to different destinations.

Redirection Operators – Your Flow Control Tools

Redirection is achieved using special symbols called **redirection operators**:
- **>** **(greater than)**: Redirects standard output to a file, overwriting the file if it exists.
- **>>** **(double greater than)**: Redirects standard output to a file, appending the output to the end of the file if it exists.
- **2>**: Redirects standard error to a file, overwriting the file if it exists.

These operators act like switches, changing the direction of the data flow and allowing you to capture command output in files, combine streams, or discard unwanted information.

Why Redirect?

Redirection is a valuable tool for several reasons:
- **Saving Command Output**: You can capture the results of a command in a file for later reference or processing. This is useful for creating reports, logs, or data sets for further analysis.
- **Creating Files**: Redirection can be used to create new files by directing output to a non-existent filename.
- **Combining Output**: You can combine the output of multiple commands into a single file by using redirection operators in sequence or within a script.
- **Controlling Error Messages**: Redirecting standard error allows you to separate error messages from normal output, making it easier to identify and troubleshoot problems.
- **Cleaning Up Output**: You can discard unwanted output or error messages by redirecting them to a special file called **/dev/null**, often referred to as the "bit bucket".

In the following sections, we'll explore how to use these redirection operators to tame the output of your commands and control the flow of information like a master conductor.

3. Redirecting Standard Input – Feeding the Stream

While we've focused on controlling the output of commands, we can also manipulate the input stream, providing data to commands from files instead of the keyboard.

< – Drawing Input from a File

The < operator redirects the standard input of a command to come from a specified file, rather than the keyboard. This allows you to feed data into a command that would normally expect interactive input.

For example, the wc (word count) command typically reads text from standard input and displays the number of lines, words, and bytes:

```
[noah@linux_lab ~]$ wc
This is a test.
^D
      1       4      16
```

In this example, we typed a line of text followed by Ctrl+D to signal the end of input. wc then processed the text and displayed the counts.

Now, let's redirect the input to come from a file named *data.txt*:

```
[noah@linux_lab ~]$ wc < data.txt
```

This command will read the contents of data.txt and display the word count results.

Applications of Input Redirection

Redirecting standard input is useful for:
- **Processing data from files**: You can feed data into commands like grep, sort, or sed for filtering, sorting, or text manipulation.
- **Automating tasks**: Scripts can use input redirection to process data from files without requiring manual input.
- **Testing commands**: You can use prepared input files to test the behavior of commands with specific data sets.

4. Redirecting Standard Output – Capturing the Essence

The standard output stream, as we learned, is the default destination for a command's normal output. By using redirection, we can capture this output and store it in a file, rather than letting it scroll past on the terminal screen.

> – Redirecting and Overwriting

The > operator redirects the standard output of a command to a specified file. If the file already exists, its contents will be overwritten with the new output.

```
[noah@linux_lab ~]$ ls -l > file_list.txt
```

This command creates the file file_list.txt (or overwrites it if it already exists) and stores the detailed directory listing within it.

>> – Appending to the File

If you want to add the output to the end of an existing file, rather than overwriting it, use the >> operator:

```
[noah@linux_lab ~]$ echo "This is a new line of text." >> file_list.txt
```

This command appends the string "This is a new line of text." to the end of the file_list.txt file.

Capturing Output from Various Commands

You can redirect the output of any command that produces standard output. Here are a few examples:

- `date > current_date.txt`: Saves the current date and time to a file.
- `df -h > disk_usage.txt`: Stores a summary of disk usage information.
- `grep "error" logfile.txt >> error_log.txt`: Extracts lines containing the word "error" from *logfile.txt* and appends them to *error_log.txt*.

By redirecting standard output, you can capture the essence of a command's results and store it for later use or analysis. This is a powerful technique for creating reports, logs, and data sets for further processing.

5. Redirecting Standard Error – Taming the Unruly

While standard output carries the desired results of a command, standard error is the channel for error messages, warnings, and diagnostic information. Redirecting standard error allows you to separate these messages from normal output, making it easier to identify and troubleshoot problems or keep a clean record of command execution.

2> – Guiding Error Messages to a File

The **2>** operator specifically redirects the standard error stream to a designated file. Similar to **>**, it will overwrite the destination file if it exists.

For example, let's attempt to list the contents of a non-existent directory and capture the resulting error message:

```
[noah@linux_lab ~]$ ls -l non_existent_directory 2> error.log
```

In this case, the error message is not displayed on the terminal; instead, it is redirected to the file error.log.

Separating Concerns

Redirecting standard error is particularly useful when you want to:

- **Keep a clean record of command output**: By separating error messages, you can maintain a clear and concise log of the command's results without cluttering it with diagnostics.
- **Troubleshoot issues**: Capturing error messages in a file allows you to analyze them later, providing clues for identifying and resolving problems.
- **Silence error messages**: In certain situations, you might want to suppress error messages from being displayed on the screen. Redirecting them to **/dev/null** effectively silences them.

Examples of Taming the Unruly

Here are a few examples of redirecting standard error:

- `grep "pattern" file.txt 2> grep_errors.log`: Searches for "pattern" in *file.txt* and redirects any error messages (e.g., if the file doesn't exist) to grep_errors.log.
- `./myscript.sh 2> /dev/null`: Runs the script *myscript.sh* and discards any error messages it might produce.

By taming the unruly standard error stream, you gain greater control over the information displayed on your terminal and create cleaner and more organized logs and outputs.

6. Combining and Discarding Streams – The Art of Control

With the ability to redirect standard output and standard error individually, you might wonder how to manage both streams simultaneously. Fortunately, the shell provides techniques for combining and discarding streams, giving you ultimate control over the flow of information.

Redirecting Both Streams

There are two primary methods for redirecting both standard output and standard error to the same file:

- **&> (Bash 4.0 and later)**: This concise operator redirects both streams to the specified file. For example:

```
[noah@linux_lab ~]$ find / -name "myfile.txt" &> search_results.txt
```

This command searches for the file *myfile.txt* throughout the entire file system and redirects both the search results and any potential error messages (e.g., permission denied errors) to the file *search_results.txt*.

- **> and 2>&1 (Traditional method)**: This method involves two separate redirections. First, standard output is redirected to the file, and then standard error is redirected to the same location as standard output (which is now the file). For example:

```
[noah@linux_lab ~]$ find / -name "myfile.txt" > search_results.txt 2>&1
```

Important Note: The order of redirections is crucial. The `2>&1` redirection must come after the `>` redirection for it to work correctly.

The Bit Bucket – /dev/null

Sometimes, you simply want to discard unwanted output or error messages, sending them into oblivion. The /dev/null device file acts as a "bit bucket," accepting input and doing absolutely nothing with it. It's like a black hole for information, making it vanish without a trace.

To discard standard output:

```
[noah@linux_lab ~]$ cat non_existent_file > /dev/null
```

To discard standard error:

```
[noah@linux_lab ~]$ ./myscript.sh 2> /dev/null
```

Orchestrating the Flow

By combining these techniques, you can achieve fine-grained control over the flow of information:

- **Capture only standard output**: `command > output.txt`
- **Capture only standard error**: `command 2> error.log`
- **Capture both streams in separate files**: `command > output.txt 2> error.log`
- **Capture both streams in the same file**: `command &> combined.txt` or `command > combined.txt 2>&1`
- **Discard standard output**: `command > /dev/null`
- **Discard standard error**: `command 2> /dev/null`

Mastering the art of combining and discarding streams empowers you to tailor the output of your commands to your specific needs, creating clean, organized, and informative results.

7. Redirection Pitfalls – Navigating the Rapids

While redirection empowers you to control the flow of information, it's essential to navigate the potential rapids and avoid mishaps that could lead to unintended consequences.

Overwriting with Care

The › redirection operator is unforgiving – it will overwrite the contents of an existing file without warning. A simple typo or a moment of forgetfulness could result in the loss of valuable data.

For example, imagine you have a file named *report.txt* containing important information, and you accidentally execute:

```
[noah@linux_lab ~]$ ls -l > report.txt
```

Your precious report would be replaced with the directory listing, leaving you with a sense of regret and a data recovery challenge.

The "Clobber" Conundrum

Overwriting files with redirection is often referred to as "clobbering." To prevent accidental clobbering, the shell provides a safeguard in the form of the noclobber option. You can enable this option using the set command:

```
[noah@linux_lab ~]$ set -o noclobber
```

With noclobber enabled, the shell will prevent redirections from overwriting existing files:

```
[noah@linux_lab ~]$ echo "New content" > report.txt
-bash: report.txt: cannot overwrite existing file
```

To override noclobber for a specific redirection, you can use the ›| operator:

```
[noah@linux_lab ~]$ echo "New content" >| report.txt
```

This will force the redirection to overwrite the file, even with noclobber enabled. However, use this with caution and only when you're certain you want to replace the existing file.

Double-Check Before You Redirect

Here are some best practices to avoid redirection mishaps:

- Always double-check your commands before pressing Enter. Make sure you're redirecting to the intended file and not accidentally overwriting something important.
- Use the `ls` command to verify the existence and contents of files before redirecting to them.
- Consider using the `noclobber` option to prevent accidental overwrites, especially when working with critical files.
- Be mindful of the order of redirections when redirecting multiple streams.

By navigating these potential pitfalls with care and awareness, you can harness the power of redirection safely and effectively.

Chapter Summary

In this chapter, we've learned to tame the flow of information on the command line like seasoned plumbers, directing input and output streams to our desired destinations:

- We explored the concept of standard streams – standard input, standard output, and standard error – and how commands interact with these streams to receive input and produce output.
- We mastered the art of redirection, using operators like `>` and `>>` to capture standard output in files, `2>` to redirect standard error, and `<` to feed input from files.
- We discovered techniques for combining and discarding streams, allowing us to control the flow of information with precision and flexibility.
- We navigated potential pitfalls, such as accidentally overwriting files with redirection, and learned how to use safeguards like the `noclobber` option.

Redirection is a fundamental skill for any command line user, enabling you to manage the output of your commands, create files, and automate tasks with scripts. As you continue your journey, you'll find countless applications for redirection, making your command line experience more efficient and productive.

In the next chapter, we'll explore the powerful concept of pipelines, learning how to chain commands together to perform complex data processing tasks.

Chapter 6:
Permission Protocols

In the collaborative world of Linux, where multiple users and processes share the same system resources, maintaining order and security is paramount. Imagine a bustling city without traffic lights or law enforcement – chaos would ensue. Similarly, without proper access control mechanisms, your Linux system would be vulnerable to unauthorized access, data breaches, and potential mayhem.

This chapter delves into the realm of **permission protocols**, the rules and regulations that govern access to files and directories. You'll learn how to decipher the secret code of file permissions, wield the `chmod` command like a master locksmith, and understand the subtle art of ownership and group membership. By mastering these access control techniques, you'll become a guardian of your digital domain, ensuring the safety and integrity of your valuable data.

1. Access Control – Guardians of the Digital Realm

Imagine a castle with fortified walls, guarded gates, and vigilant sentries. The security of the castle depends on controlling who can enter, where they can go, and what actions they can perform. Similarly, **access control** in the Linux file system safeguards your data by defining who can access files and directories and what operations they are permitted to perform.

The Importance of Access Control

In a multi-user environment like Linux, where multiple users and processes share the same system resources, access control is crucial for several reasons:
- **Data Protection**: Access control mechanisms prevent unauthorized users from viewing, modifying, or deleting sensitive information. This is essential for maintaining the privacy and integrity of your personal files, confidential documents, and system-critical data.
- **System Stability**: Restricting access to system files and directories ensures that only authorized users (typically the system administrator) can make changes that could affect the stability and security of the operating system.
- **Collaboration and Sharing**: Access control allows you to selectively share files and directories with other users, fostering collaboration while still maintaining control over who can access and modify shared data.
- **Preventing Accidental Damage**: By limiting access and permissions, you can prevent accidental deletion or modification of important files, protecting your data from unintended harm.

The Guardians of Your Data

The primary mechanisms for access control in Linux are:
- **File Permissions**: Define what actions (read, write, execute) are permitted for different categories of users (owner, group, others).
- **File Ownership**: Determines who "owns" the file and has primary control over its permissions and attributes.
- **Group Ownership**: Allows for shared access among a group of users.

In the following sections, we'll explore these mechanisms in detail, equipping you with the knowledge and tools to become a vigilant guardian of your digital realm.

2. Users, Groups, and Others – The Access Hierarchy

Imagine a kingdom with a king, his loyal knights, and the common folk. Each group has different roles and privileges within the kingdom's hierarchy. Similarly, the Linux file system has a hierarchy of access, defining who can interact with files and directories and to what extent.

- **File Ownership – The King and His Domain**: Every file and directory in Linux belongs to a specific **owner**, typically the user who created it. The owner is like the king of the file, holding the highest level of control and privileges. They can read, write, execute, and modify the file's permissions as they see fit.
- **Group Ownership – The Knights of the Round Table**: Files and directories also belong to a **group**. The group is like a band of knights, sharing certain privileges and responsibilities. The owner can grant specific permissions to the group, allowing its members to access and interact with the file in a controlled manner.
- **Others – The Common Folk**: Beyond the owner and the group lies the realm of **others**, often referred to as the world. This encompasses all other users on the system who are not the owner or members of the group. The owner can assign a set of permissions for others, determining what level of access, if any, they have to the file.

Identifying Yourself and Your Allies

To view information about your user identity and group memberships, use the `id` command:

```
[noah@linux_lab ~]$ id
uid=1000(noah) gid=1000(noah) groups=1000(noah)
```

This output tells us that the current user is "noah" with a user ID (uid) of 1000. The user also belongs to a group named "noah" with a group ID (gid) of 1000. In this case, the user only belongs to their primary group, but it's possible for users to be members of multiple groups, expanding their access and collaboration capabilities.

The Hierarchy of Access

The access hierarchy in Linux, with the owner at the top, followed by the group and then others, provides a structured and flexible way to manage file permissions. It allows for granular control over who can access files and directories and what actions they can perform, ensuring data security and facilitating collaboration in a multi-user environment.

3. File Permission Modes – The Access Code

Just as a combination lock requires the correct sequence of numbers to grant access, files and directories in Linux have permission modes that act as access codes, determining who can enter and what actions they can perform. These permission modes are like a secret language, encoded within the file system and revealed through the output of the `ls -l` command.

Deciphering the Permission String

When you use `ls -l` to view a detailed directory listing, you'll see a string of ten characters representing the file's mode or permissions:

```
[noah@linux_lab ~]$ ls -l notes.txt
-rw-rw-r-- 1 noah noah 765 Oct 27 10:32 notes.txt
```

Let's break down the meaning of these characters:
- **File Type**: The first character indicates the type of file: - for a regular file, **d** for a directory, and **l** for a symbolic link.
- **Owner Permissions**: The next three characters represent the permissions for the file's owner: **r** for read, **w** for write, and **x** for execute. A hyphen (-) means the permission is not granted. In our example, the owner has read and write permissions but not execute permissions.
- **Group Permissions**: The next three characters represent the permissions for the group that owns the file. In our example, the group also has read and write permissions.
- **Others Permissions**: The final three characters represent the permissions for all other users on the system. In our example, others only have read permissions.

Understanding Permission Bits

Each permission (**r**, **w**, **x**) corresponds to a specific action:
- **Read (r)**: Allows viewing the contents of a file or listing the contents of a directory.
- **Write (w)**: Allows modifying the contents of a file or creating, deleting, and renaming files within a directory.

67

- **Execute (x):** Allows executing a file as a program or entering a directory with cd.

Examples of Permission Modes

Here are some examples of common permission modes and their implications:
- -rw-------: The file is only readable and writable by the owner. No one else has any access.
- -rwx------: The file is readable, writable, and executable by the owner. Again, no access for anyone else.
- -rw-r--r--: The owner can read and write the file. The group and others can only read the file.
- -rwxr-xr-x: The owner has full access (read, write, execute). The group and others can read and execute the file but cannot modify it.
- drwxr-xr-x: This is a directory where the owner has full access, and the group and others have read and execute permissions, allowing them to list the directory contents and enter the directory.

Understanding file permission modes is essential for managing access control and ensuring the security and integrity of your data. In the next section, we'll explore how to modify these permissions using the chmod command.

4. chmod – The Permission Modifier

The chmod command, short for "change mode," is your tool for modifying file permissions, granting or revoking access like a master locksmith adjusting the tumblers of a lock. chmod offers two distinct methods for specifying permission changes: octal notation and symbolic notation.

Octal Notation – The Numerical Code

Octal notation uses a three-digit octal number to represent the permissions for the owner, group, and others. Each digit corresponds to a set of three permission bits (read, write, execute), as shown in the following table:

Octal Digit	Binary Equivalent	Permissions
0	000	--- (no permissions)
1	001	--x (execute only)
2	010	-w- (write only)
3	011	-wx (write and execute)

4	100	r-- (read only)
5	101	r-x (read and execute)
6	110	rw- (read and write)
7	111	rwx (read, write, and execute)

To use octal notation, type `chmod` followed by the three-digit octal number and the filename:

```
[noah@linux_lab ~]$ chmod 644 myfile.txt
```

This command sets the permissions for *myfile.txt* to `rw-r--r--`, granting read and write permissions to the owner and read-only permissions to the group and others.

Symbolic Notation – The Human-Readable Code

Symbolic notation provides a more human-readable way to specify permission changes. It uses a combination of letters and symbols to represent user categories, operations, and permissions:

- **User Categories**:
    - `u` - user (owner)
    - `g` - group
    - `o` - others
    - `a` - all (owner, group, and others)
- **Operators**:
    - `+` - add permission
    - `-` - remove permission
    - `=` - set exact permissions
- **Permissions**:
    - `r` - read
    - `w` - write
    - `x` - execute

For example, to add execute permission for the owner of *script.sh*:

```
[noah@linux_lab ~]$ chmod u+x script.sh
```

To remove write permission for the group:

```
[noah@linux_lab ~]$ chmod g-w script.sh
```

To set the permissions for others to read-only:

69

```
[noah@linux_lab ~]$ chmod o=r script.sh
```

Choosing Your Notation

Both octal and symbolic notation have their advantages. Octal notation is concise and efficient, while symbolic notation is more intuitive and easier to remember. Choose the notation that best suits your style and the task at hand.

With `chmod` in your command line toolkit, you have the power to fine-tune file permissions and control access to your data with precision and confidence.

5. umask – Setting the Default Stage

Imagine a theater director setting the stage for a play, arranging the props and scenery before the actors arrive. The `umask` command in Linux plays a similar role, establishing the default permissions for newly created files and directories, setting the stage for their access and usage.

The umask Mask – A Permission Template

The `umask` is a mask that determines which permission bits are not granted by default to newly created files and directories. It's like a stencil that blocks out certain permissions, leaving only the desired ones visible.

Viewing the Current umask

To view the current `umask` setting, use the `umask` command without any arguments:

```
[noah@linux_lab ~]$ umask
0022
```

The output `0022` is an octal number representing the permission mask.

Interpreting the Mask

Let's decode the meaning of the `0022` mask:
- The first digit (0) applies to special permission bits, which we'll discuss later. For now, we can ignore it.
- The second digit (0) represents the owner's permissions. A value of 0 means no permissions are masked from the default for files (666) and directories (777).

- The third digit (2) represents the permissions for the group and others. A value of 2 (which is 010 in binary) means the write permission bit is masked. Therefore, with a `umask` of 0022, new files will have permissions of 644 (`rw-r--r--`) and new directories will have permissions of 755 (`rwxr-xr-x`).

Setting the umask

To set a new `umask`, use the `umask` command followed by the desired octal mask:

```
[noah@linux_lab ~]$ umask 0002
```

This command sets the mask to `0002`, which means that newly created files and directories will have read and write permissions for the owner and group and read-only permission for others.

The Default Stage for Access Control

The `umask` command plays a crucial role in establishing the default access control settings for your files and directories. By understanding how to interpret and set the umask, you can ensure that new files and directories are created with appropriate permissions, maintaining security and control over your data.

6. Special Permissions – Beyond the Basics

In addition to the standard read, write, and execute permissions, the Linux file system offers a set of special permissions that provide more nuanced control over file access and execution. These **special permissions**, like hidden switches, can modify the behavior of files and directories in unique ways.

The Trio of Special Permissions

There are three primary special permissions:
- **setuid (set user ID)**: When set on an executable file, it allows the user executing the file to temporarily inherit the privileges of the file's owner during execution. This is often used for system administration commands that require elevated privileges but need to be accessible to regular users.
- **setgid (set group ID)**: Similar to setuid, but it grants the user executing the file the effective group ID of the file's group owner during execution. This can be used to allow users to access files and resources that are restricted to a specific group.

- **sticky bit**: When applied to a directory, the sticky bit restricts the deletion and renaming of files within the directory. Only the file's owner, the directory owner, or the superuser can remove or rename files, even if other users have write permissions to the directory. This is often used for shared directories like /tmp to prevent users from interfering with each other's files.

Viewing Special Permissions

When you use ls -l, special permissions are indicated by a letter in the execute position for the respective user category (owner, group, others):
- **setuid**: s in the owner's execute position (e.g., -rwsr-xr-x)
- **setgid**: s in the group's execute position (e.g., -rw-r-sr--)
- **sticky bit**: t in the others' execute position (e.g., -rwxrwxrwt)

Setting Special Permissions

You can set special permissions using the chmod command with symbolic notation:
- **setuid**: chmod u+s filename
- **setgid**: chmod g+s filename
- **sticky bit**: chmod +t directory_name

Uses of Special Permissions

Here are a few examples of how special permissions are used:
- The passwd command is setuid root, allowing regular users to change their passwords, which requires modifying the /etc/shadow file (typically only accessible by the root user).
- A shared project directory might be setgid to a specific group, ensuring that all files created within the directory belong to that group, facilitating collaboration among team members.
- The /tmp directory often has the sticky bit set to prevent users from deleting or renaming files that belong to other users.

By understanding and utilizing special permissions, you can achieve finer-grained control over file access and execution, enhancing security and collaboration within your Linux system.

7. Changing Ownership – Transferring Control

Just as a property deed transfers ownership of a house, the `chown` and `chgrp` commands allow you to change the ownership of files and directories in Linux, transferring control and privileges to different users and groups.

chown – The Ownership Granter

The `chown` command, short for "change owner," modifies both the user owner and group owner of a file or directory. It requires superuser privileges to execute, as changing ownership can have significant implications for file access and security.

The basic syntax is:

```
chown owner:group file...
```

Here are a few examples:
- **Change owner to "user1"**: `sudo chown user1 myfile.txt`
- **Change group owner to "staff"**: `sudo chown :staff myfile.txt`
- **Change both owner and group owner**: `sudo chown user1:staff myfile.txt`

chgrp – Focusing on the Group

The `chgrp` command, short for "change group," specifically changes the group ownership of a file or directory. Like `chown`, it requires superuser privileges:

```
chgrp group file...
```

For example:

```
[noah@linux_lab ~]$ sudo chgrp project_team project.tgz
```

This command changes the group owner of project.tgz to the group named "project_team".

Transferring Control – Use Cases

Changing ownership is often necessary in situations such as:
- **Collaboration**: When multiple users are working on a project, it might be necessary to transfer ownership of files or directories to ensure that everyone has the appropriate access and permissions.

- **System Administration**: The system administrator might need to change ownership of files or directories for maintenance or security purposes.
- **File Transfers**: When files are transferred between systems or users, it's often necessary to adjust ownership to reflect the new environment.

A Word of Caution

Changing ownership can have significant consequences for file access and security. Always exercise caution and ensure that you understand the implications before transferring control of files or directories.

8. The Principle of Least Privilege – Security Best Practices

Imagine a fortress with multiple layers of defense, each guarded by soldiers with specific roles and responsibilities. The outer walls might be patrolled by archers, while the inner sanctum is protected by the king's elite guard. This layered approach ensures that access is granted only to those who need it, minimizing the risk of breaches and intrusions. Similarly, the **principle of least privilege** is a fundamental security best practice that advocates granting users and processes the minimum level of access necessary to perform their tasks.

Minimizing Risk with Minimal Permissions

By adhering to the principle of least privilege, you reduce the potential attack surface of your system, mitigating risks in several ways:
- **Reduced Impact of Errors**: If a user or process accidentally executes a command or modifies a file with overly broad permissions, the potential for damage is limited.
- **Containment of Breaches**: If a user account or process is compromised, the attacker's ability to inflict damage is restricted by the limited permissions associated with that account or process.
- **Improved System Stability**: Preventing unauthorized modifications to system files and configurations reduces the risk of system instability and crashes.

Best Practices for Permission Management

Here are some recommendations for implementing the principle of least privilege:

- **Create user accounts with minimal privileges**: Regular users should not have access to system files or administrative commands.
- **Use groups to manage shared access**: Create groups for specific purposes and assign permissions accordingly. This allows for controlled collaboration without granting excessive access to individual users.
- **Grant temporary privileges with** `sudo`: Instead of giving users permanent superuser access, use `sudo` to allow them to execute specific commands with elevated privileges when needed.
- **Regularly review and audit permissions**: Periodically check file and directory permissions to ensure they align with the principle of least privilege.
- **Be mindful of default permissions**: Pay attention to the `umask` setting and adjust it as needed to ensure that new files and directories are created with appropriate permissions.
- **Use caution with special permissions**: setuid, setgid, and the sticky bit are powerful tools, but they should be used sparingly and only when necessary.

By adopting these best practices and embracing the principle of least privilege, you can create a more secure and resilient Linux environment, protecting your data and systems from unauthorized access and potential harm.

Chapter Summary

In this chapter, we've donned the mantle of security experts, learning the art of access control and becoming guardians of our digital realms:

- We explored the importance of file permissions and ownership in a multi-user environment, understanding how they protect data and maintain system stability.
- We learned about the access hierarchy – owner, group, and others – and how it defines levels of access and control.
- We deciphered the permission mode strings displayed by `ls -l`, understanding the meaning of each permission bit and how they control file and directory access.
- We became masters of `chmod`, wielding both octal and symbolic notation to modify file permissions with precision.
- We explored the `umask` command and its role in setting the default permissions for newly created files and directories.

- We uncovered the secrets of special permission bits – setuid, setgid, and the sticky bit – and their uses for advanced access control scenarios.
- We learned how to transfer ownership of files and directories using the `chown` and `chgrp` commands.
- We embraced the principle of least privilege, adopting best practices for managing permissions and minimizing security risks.

Remember, access control is essential for maintaining a secure and stable Linux environment. By applying the principles and techniques covered in this chapter, you can confidently manage permissions, protect your data, and ensure that your system remains a well-guarded fortress.

Part 2:
Mastering Text
Manipulation

Chapter 7:
Piping and Filtering Data

Imagine a series of water purification stages, each refining and transforming the water as it flows through the system. In the realm of the Linux command line, **pipelines** offer a similar mechanism for processing data. They allow you to chain commands together, passing the output of one command as input to the next, creating a powerful flow of data manipulation.

The key to building these pipelines lies in the concept of **filters**. Filters are commands specifically designed to process and modify data, typically reading from standard input and writing their results to standard output. In this chapter, we'll explore a collection of commonly used filters, such as `grep`, `sort`, and `uniq`, and learn how to combine them into pipelines to achieve remarkable feats of text processing and data manipulation. So, let's embark on this journey of data transformation and unlock the power of pipelines!

1. Pipelines – Connecting the Dots

The Linux command line is not just about executing isolated commands; it's about creating connections and building workflows. **Pipelines** are the conduits that enable this interconnectedness, allowing you to channel the output of one command directly into the input of another.

The Pipe Operator – The Bridge Between Commands

The pipe operator (|) is the cornerstone of pipelines. It acts as a bridge, connecting the standard output (stdout) of the command on its left to the standard input (stdin) of the command on its right.

```
command1 | command2
```

Imagine a stream of data flowing from `command1`, passing through the pipe, and entering `command2` for further processing. This elegant mechanism allows you to combine the strengths of multiple commands, creating a powerful chain of data manipulation.

Visualizing the Flow

Let's illustrate the flow of data through a simple pipeline:

```
[noah@linux_lab ~]$ ls -l | less
```

- The `ls -l` command generates a detailed listing of files and directories, sending its output to standard output.
- The pipe operator (|) intercepts this output and redirects it to the standard input of the `less` command.
- The `less` command receives the directory listing as input and displays it in a paginated format, allowing you to scroll through the results one page at a time.

In this example, the pipeline combines the capabilities of `ls -l` and `less`, providing a more convenient way to view a potentially long directory listing.

The Power of Connection

Pipelines offer numerous advantages:

- **Efficiency**: Instead of manually saving the output of one command and then using it as input for another, pipelines streamline the process, allowing for efficient data flow.
- **Flexibility**: You can combine commands in countless ways to achieve complex tasks, tailoring the data processing to your specific needs.
- **Modularity**: Pipelines promote a modular approach to problem-solving, allowing you to break down complex tasks into smaller, more manageable steps.

In the next section, we'll explore the concept of **filters**, the specialized commands that form the building blocks of most pipelines.

2. Filters – Transforming the Stream

Pipelines are powerful conduits, but the magic truly happens within the commands that process the data as it flows through the system. These specialized commands, known as **filters**, are the workhorses of text processing and data manipulation.

The Essence of a Filter

A filter is a command that typically exhibits the following characteristics:
- **Reads from standard input**: Filters are designed to accept input from the standard input stream (stdin), allowing them to receive data from a pipe or redirection.
- **Processes the data**: Filters perform some operation on the input data, such as searching, sorting, or transforming text.
- **Writes to standard output**: Filters send their processed output to the standard output stream (stdout), making it available for further processing in a pipeline or redirection to a file.

Common Filtering Operations

Filters come in a wide variety, each with its own unique capabilities. Here are a few common filtering operations:
- **Searching**: Finding specific patterns or lines of text within a data stream (e.g., `grep`).
- **Sorting**: Ordering data based on specific criteria (e.g., `sort`).
- **Transforming**: Modifying the format or content of the data (e.g., `tr`, `sed`).
- **Selecting**: Extracting specific portions of the data (e.g., `cut`, `head`, `tail`).

- **Counting**: Determining the number of lines, words, or other units in the data (e.g., `wc`).

A Symphony of Transformation

By combining multiple filters in a pipeline, you can achieve complex data transformations, orchestrating a symphony of processing steps.

For example, imagine you have a text file containing a list of names, and you want to extract the last names, sort them alphabetically, and remove any duplicates. You could achieve this with the following pipeline:

```
cut -d ' ' -f 2 names.txt | sort | uniq
```

In this pipeline, the `cut` command extracts the second field (last names) from each line, the `sort` command orders the last names alphabetically, and finally, `uniq` removes any duplicates, producing a clean and sorted list of unique last names.

In the upcoming sections, we'll explore several commonly used filters and their options, preparing you to build your own data processing pipelines.

3. grep – The Master Text Searcher

Within the vast ocean of text data, finding specific information can feel like searching for a needle in a haystack. The `grep` command, like a powerful magnet, allows you to extract lines of text that match a specified pattern, making it an invaluable tool for searching and filtering data.

Searching with Patterns

`grep` uses **regular expressions (regex)** or fixed strings to define search patterns. In its basic form, you provide `grep` with a pattern and one or more files to search:

```
grep pattern file…
```

For instance, to find lines containing the word "error" in a file named logfile.txt:

```
[noah@linux_lab ~]$ grep "error" logfile.txt
```

This command will display any lines in logfile.txt where the word "error" appears.

grep Options – Refining the Search

`grep` offers a variety of options to fine-tune your search:
- `-i` **(ignore case)**: Makes the search case-insensitive, matching both uppercase and lowercase letters.
- `-v` **(invert match)**: Displays lines that do not match the pattern.
- `-c` **(count)**: Prints only the count of matching lines, rather than the lines themselves.
- `-n` **(line number)**: Prefixes each matching line with its line number in the file.

Grep in Pipelines – Filtering the Flow

`grep` is a powerful filter in pipelines, allowing you to extract specific lines from the output of other commands. For example, to find processes named "firefox" and display their process IDs (PIDs):

```
[noah@linux_lab ~]$ ps aux | grep firefox | grep -v grep | awk '{print $2}'
```

This pipeline demonstrates several concepts:
- `ps aux`: Lists all running processes.
- `grep firefox`: Filters the process list, keeping only lines containing "firefox".
- `grep -v grep`: Removes the line corresponding to the `grep` command itself, as it would also match the search pattern.
- `awk '{print $2}'`: Extracts the second field (PID) from the remaining lines.

The Master of Text Search

`grep`'s ability to search for patterns makes it a versatile and powerful tool for a wide range of tasks, from finding specific information in log files and configuration files to filtering data and extracting relevant content from text streams.

4. sort – Ordering the Chaos

In a world of information overload, order and organization are essential for making sense of data. The `sort` command, like a meticulous librarian, arranges lines of text into a specific order, bringing structure and clarity to your data sets.

Sorting Lines

The `sort` command reads data from files or standard input and outputs the lines in a specified order. In its simplest form, it sorts lines alphabetically:

```
[noah@linux_lab ~]$ cat words.txt
apple
banana
cherry
date
[noah@linux_lab ~]$ sort words.txt
apple
banana
cherry
date
```

In this example, the lines in words.txt are already in alphabetical order, so `sort` produces the same output. However, if the lines were jumbled, `sort` would arrange them correctly.

Sort Options – Customizing the Order

`sort` offers a variety of options to tailor the sorting behavior:
- **-r (reverse)**: Sorts in reverse order, from Z to A or from highest to lowest numerically.
- **-n (numeric)**: Sorts lines numerically, comparing the numerical values of the text.
- **-k (key)**: Sorts based on a specific field or column within each line. You can specify the field number and sorting options for that field. For example, `-k 2,2n` would sort numerically based on the second field.
- **-t (field separator)**: Defines the character used to separate fields in the input. The default separator is whitespace (spaces or tabs).

Sorting in Pipelines – Bringing Order to the Flow

`sort` is a valuable filter in pipelines, allowing you to organize data before further processing. For example, to sort a list of processes by their memory usage:

```
[noah@linux_lab ~]$ ps aux | sort -k 4nr | head
```

This pipeline demonstrates several concepts:
1. `ps aux`: Lists all running processes.
2. `sort -k 4nr`: Sorts numerically (-n) in reverse order (-r) based on the fourth field (-k 4), which represents memory usage.
3. `head`: Displays the first few lines of the sorted output, showing the processes with the highest memory usage.

Bringing Order to the Data

The `sort` command, with its various options and ability to work within pipelines, is an essential tool for organizing and analyzing data, whether you're working with simple lists, tabular data, or complex datasets.

5. uniq – Eliminating Redundancy

Imagine a cluttered closet where you find multiple copies of the same shirt, taking up valuable space. The `uniq` command, like a tidying expert, helps you eliminate redundancy in your data by removing duplicate lines from sorted files or text streams.

Removing Duplicates

The `uniq` command analyzes a sorted input and removes adjacent duplicate lines, outputting the unique lines to standard output. It's important to note that the input must be sorted for `uniq` to work effectively.

For example, let's say you have a file named *colors.txt* with the following content:

```
red
blue
green
red
blue
yellow
```

To identify the unique colors, you would first sort the file and then pipe the output to `uniq`:

```
[noah@linux_lab ~]$ sort colors.txt | uniq
blue
```

```
green
red
yellow
```

uniq Options – Fine-Tuning Duplication Detection

`uniq` offers several options to customize its behavior:
- `-c` **(count)**: Displays each unique line along with the number of times it appeared consecutively in the input.
- `-d` **(repeated)**: Displays only the lines that have duplicates, showing each duplicate line only once.
- `-u` **(unique)**: Displays only lines that are unique, omitting any lines that have duplicates.
- `-i` **(ignore case)**: Ignores case distinctions when comparing lines.

uniq in Pipelines – Streamlining Redundancy Removal

`uniq` often works in conjunction with `sort` within pipelines to streamline the process of identifying or removing duplicates. For example, to display the number of occurrences of each word in a text file:

```
[noah@linux_lab ~]$ cat words.txt
apple banana orange apple strawberry apple banana pear apple cherry grape strawberry
banana apple orange pear banana strawberry cherry apple orange
[noah@linux_lab ~]$ cat words.txt | tr ' ' '\n' | sort | uniq -c
      6 apple
      4 banana
      2 cherry
      1 grape
      3 orange
      2 pear
      3 strawberry
```

This pipeline demonstrates several steps:
1. **cat words.txt**: Reads the content of the file.
2. **tr ' ' '\n'**: Replaces spaces with newlines, turning each word into a separate line.
3. **sort**: Sorts the words alphabetically.
4. **uniq -c**: Counts the occurrences of each unique word and displays the results.

The Power of Uniqueness

By eliminating redundancy, `uniq` helps you focus on the unique elements within your data, making it a valuable tool for analyzing data sets, cleaning up lists, and identifying patterns.

6. wc – Counting the Words (and Lines and Bytes)

The `wc` command, short for "word count," is a simple yet versatile tool for counting lines, words, and bytes in files or text streams. It's like having a digital abacus, providing quick statistics about the size and composition of your textual data.

Counting with wc

In its basic form, `wc` displays the number of lines, words, and bytes in the specified file:

```
[noah@linux_lab ~]$ wc words.txt
   1     21     148 words.txt
```

This output indicates that *words.txt* contains 1 lines, 21 words, and 148 bytes of data.

wc Options – Focusing the Count

wc offers options to focus the count on specific aspects:
- -l **(lines)**: Displays only the number of lines.
- -w **(words)**: Displays only the number of words.
- -c **(bytes)**: Displays only the number of bytes.

For example, to count the number of lines in a file:

```
[noah@linux_lab ~]$ wc -l words.txt
11 words.txt
```

Counting in Pipelines – Measuring the Flow

`wc` is often used within pipelines to measure the flow of data. For instance, to count the number of files in a directory:

```
[noah@linux_lab ~]$ ls -l | wc -l
```

This pipeline uses `ls -l` to produce a detailed directory listing and then pipes the output to `wc -l` to count the number of lines, which corresponds to the number of files and directories.

A Simple Tool for Data Insights

While `wc` might appear basic, it provides valuable insights into the structure and size of your data. Whether you're counting lines of code, words in a document, or bytes of data processed, `wc` is a handy tool for understanding the scope and composition of your textual information.

7. head and tail – Glimpsing the Beginning and End

Imagine you have a long scroll of parchment and you want to quickly peek at the opening lines or the closing remarks. The `head` and `tail` commands serve as your viewing lenses, allowing you to glimpse the beginning and end of text files or data streams with ease.

head – A Glimpse at the Start

The `head` command displays the first few lines of a file, providing a quick preview of its content:

```
[noah@linux_lab ~]$ head words.txt
This is an example
of a text file
with multiple
lines to
demonstrate
the use of
commands
like head
and tail.
These
```

By default, head displays the first 10 lines. You can adjust the number of lines using the -n option:

```
[noah@linux_lab ~]$ head -n 5 words.txt
This is an example
of a text file
with multiple
lines to
demonstrate
```

tail – A Peek at the End

The tail command, as its name implies, displays the last few lines of a file:

```
[noah@linux_lab ~]$ tail words.txt
demonstrate
the use of
commands
like head
and tail.
These
commands
are often
used in
pipelines.
```

Like head, tail defaults to displaying 10 lines, and you can customize the number of lines with the -n option.

Real-Time Monitoring with tail -f

tail has a special superpower: the -f (follow) option allows you to monitor a file in real-time. As new lines are added to the file, they are immediately displayed on your terminal. This is particularly useful for watching log files as they are being written:

```
[noah@linux_lab ~]$ tail -f /var/log/messages
```

This command will continuously display new entries in the system log file, providing a live view of system activity. To stop monitoring, press Ctrl+C.

Extracting Portions with head and tail

Both `head` and `tail` are valuable filters in pipelines, allowing you to extract specific portions of data streams. For example, to display lines 11 to 20 of a file:

```
[noah@linux_lab ~]$ head -n 20 words.txt | tail -n 10
```

This pipeline first extracts the first 20 lines using `head` and then pipes the result to `tail`, which displays the last 10 lines of that subset, effectively showing lines 11 to 20.

A Glimpse into the Data

`head` and `tail` provide a quick and convenient way to preview and examine the contents of files and data streams. Whether you're peeking at the beginning, the end, or watching a live stream of data, these commands offer valuable insights into your textual information.

8. Building Pipelines – The Art of Composition

With a collection of filters at your disposal, you're ready to become a pipeline composer, orchestrating the flow of data through multiple stages of processing. Building pipelines is an art that combines creativity and logic, allowing you to transform raw data into meaningful information.

The Pipeline Symphony

Let's explore a few examples of pipeline compositions:

Extracting and Sorting IP Addresses

Imagine you have a log file containing web server access logs, and you want to extract the unique IP addresses that accessed the server and sort them numerically.

```
[noah@linux_lab ~]$ cut -d ' ' -f 1 access.log | sort -n | uniq
```

This pipeline demonstrates several steps:
1. **cut -d ' ' -f 1 access.log**: Extracts the first field (IP addresses) from each line in *access.log*, assuming that the fields are delimited by spaces.
2. **sort -n**: Sorts the IP addresses numerically.

3. **uniq**: Removes any duplicate IP addresses, resulting in a sorted list of unique visitors.

Analyzing System Users

Let's say you want to find out which shells are used by users on your system and count the number of users for each shell.

```
[noah@linux_lab ~]$ cut -d ':' -f 7 /etc/passwd | sort | uniq -c
```

This pipeline performs the following steps:
1. **cut -d ':' -f 7 /etc/passwd**: Extracts the seventh field (default shell) from each line in the */etc/passwd* file, which contains user account information.
2. **sort**: Sorts the shells alphabetically.
3. **uniq -c**: Counts the number of users for each unique shell.

Filtering and Counting Error Messages

Imagine you have a log file containing system messages, and you want to count the number of error messages that occurred in the past hour.

```
[noah@linux_lab ~]$ grep "error" /var/log/messages | grep "$(date +"%b %_d")" | wc -l
```

This pipeline demonstrates the following:
1. **grep "error" /var/log/messages**: Extracts lines containing the word "error" from the system log file.
2. **grep "$(date +"%b %_d")"**: Filters the error messages, keeping only those that occurred on the current day (using the output of the date command to construct the search pattern).
3. **wc -l**: Counts the number of remaining lines, indicating the number of error messages for the day.

The Art of Data Transformation

Building pipelines is an art that requires understanding the capabilities of individual filters and how they can be combined to achieve your desired outcome. Experiment with different combinations, explore command options, and let your creativity flow as you transform raw data into meaningful insights.

As you become more comfortable with pipelines, you'll discover their power and versatility for solving a wide range of data processing challenges.

Chapter Summary

In this chapter, we've journeyed through the powerful world of pipelines and filters, learning how to connect commands and transform data with elegance and efficiency:

- We explored the concept of pipelines as a means of chaining commands together, with the pipe operator (|) acting as the bridge between standard output and standard input.
- We discovered the role of filters in data processing, understanding their ability to read from standard input, transform data, and write to standard output.
- We delved into several commonly used filters, including `grep` for searching text, `sort` for ordering data, `uniq` for removing duplicates, `wc` for counting, and `head` and `tail` for extracting specific portions of data.
- We learned the art of composing pipelines, combining multiple filters to achieve complex data transformations and extract meaningful insights from raw data.

Pipelines are a cornerstone of command line mastery, allowing you to harness the power of multiple commands and perform sophisticated data processing tasks with ease. As you continue your exploration, you'll find countless applications for pipelines, streamlining your workflow and unlocking new levels of efficiency.

In the next chapter, we'll delve even deeper into the world of text manipulation, exploring powerful tools like cut, paste, and join that allow you to slice, dice, and combine text files with precision and finesse.

Chapter 8:
Text Processing
Powerhouse

The Linux command line is not merely a realm of cryptic commands and blinking cursors; it's a playground for manipulating and transforming text data with precision and power. While basic tools like `cat` and `echo` allow you to view and create text, a set of advanced commands elevate you to the status of a text processing powerhouse.

In this chapter, we'll explore these powerful tools – `cut`, `paste`, and `join` – which will enable you to slice and dice text files, extract specific information, and combine data from multiple sources. You'll learn the art of using field delimiters to navigate structured data and discover how to create custom reports and transform text into the format you desire. So, prepare to unleash your inner data maestro and become a master of text manipulation!

1. Beyond Basic Tools – A Text Processing Powerhouse

While commands like `cat`, `echo`, and `less` allow you to view and create text, they offer limited capabilities for working with structured data, such as tables or spreadsheets. Imagine trying to extract a specific column of information from a CSV file or merging data from multiple text files using only these basic tools – the task would be tedious and error-prone.

This is where the advanced text processing tools of the Linux command line come into play. Commands like `cut`, `paste`, and `join` elevate your text manipulation skills to a whole new level, enabling you to:

- **Extract specific columns or fields from text files**: Imagine slicing a cake with perfect precision, separating the layers with ease. `cut` allows you to do the same with text files, extracting specific columns or fields based on delimiters.
- **Combine columns or files side-by-side**: `paste` acts like a skilled chef, combining ingredients from different bowls into a harmonious blend. It allows you to merge data from multiple files or columns, creating new datasets or custom reports.
- **Merge lines based on a common field**: `join` is like a matchmaker, bringing together lines from two files that share a common attribute. It's a powerful tool for combining data from related sources, such as customer records and order information.

The Role of Field Delimiters

The key to understanding these advanced text processing tools lies in the concept of field delimiters. A delimiter is a character or sequence of characters that separates individual fields or columns within a text file. Common delimiters include:

- **Spaces**: Used in many plain text files and system data files.
- **Tabs**: Often used in tabular data and spreadsheets.
- **Commas**: The standard delimiter for CSV (Comma Separated Values) files.
- **Colons**: Used in configuration files like `/etc/passwd`.

By specifying the appropriate delimiter, you can instruct these commands to identify and manipulate specific fields within your text data, unlocking a world of possibilities for data extraction, transformation, and analysis.

2. cut – The Precision Slicer

The `cut` command is your surgical knife for text processing, allowing you to extract specific sections of text from lines in files or data streams. Imagine slicing a loaf of bread into perfect, even slices – cut provides that same level of precision for your text data.

Cutting by Characters or Fields

cut offers two primary modes for specifying what to extract:
- -c (characters): Extracts sections of text based on character positions within each line.
- -f (fields): Extracts specific fields or columns based on a delimiter.

Cutting by Characters with -c

The -c option allows you to specify a list of character positions or ranges to extract. For example, to extract the first five characters from each line:

```
[noah@linux_lab ~]$ cut -c 1-5 data.txt
```

To extract characters 10 to 15 and 20 to the end of the line:

```
[noah@linux_lab ~]$ cut -c 10-15,20- data.txt
```

Cutting by Fields with -f

The -f option is ideal for working with structured data where fields are separated by delimiters. You can specify the field numbers you want to extract, separated by commas. For example, to extract the first and third fields from a comma-separated file:

```
[noah@linux_lab ~]$ cut -d ',' -f 1,3 data.csv
```

The -d option specifies the delimiter, which is a comma (,) in this case.

Delimiters – The Cutting Guides

cut supports various delimiters, allowing you to work with different types of structured data:
- **Whitespace**: The default delimiter, separating fields based on spaces or tabs.
- **Comma (,)**: Commonly used in CSV files.
- **Colon (":")**: Found in configuration files like /etc/passwd.
- **Any single character**: You can specify any character as a delimiter using the -d option.

96

Examples of cut in Action

Here are a few examples of using `cut` for data extraction:
- **Extracting usernames from /etc/passwd**: `cut -d ':' -f 1 /etc/passwd`
- **Extracting the date from a log file**: `cut -d ' ' -f 4 access.log`
- **Extracting the second column from a CSV file**: `cut -d ',' -f 2 data.csv`

The `cut` command, with its precision slicing capabilities, is an indispensable tool for working with structured data, allowing you to extract and isolate specific information from text files and data streams.

3. paste – The Side-by-Side Combiner

Imagine a master chef arranging ingredients on a plate, placing each element side-by-side to create a visually appealing and harmonious dish. The `paste` command in the Linux command line performs a similar function, merging lines from multiple files or standard input and arranging them horizontally, creating a combined output with fields neatly aligned.

Combining Lines

`paste` reads lines from one or more files and joins them together, separating the fields from each line with a specified delimiter. The basic syntax is:

```
paste file1 file2 ...
```

For example, let's say you have two files: *names.txt* containing a list of first names and *lastnames.txt* containing a list of last names:

```
[noah@linux_lab ~]$ cat names.txt
Alice
Bob
Charlie
[noah@linux_lab ~]$ cat lastnames.txt
Smith
Jones
Brown
```

To combine these files, creating a list of full names:

```
[noah@linux_lab ~]$ paste names.txt lastnames.txt
Alice Smith
Bob Jones
Charlie Brown
```

Delimiters – Aligning the Ingredients

By default, paste uses a tab character as the delimiter between fields. You can specify a different delimiter using the -d option:

```
[noah@linux_lab ~]$ paste -d ',' names.txt lastnames.txt
Alice,Smith
Bob,Jones
Charlie,Brown
```

Serial Merging with -s

The -s option instructs paste to merge files serially, placing lines from each file below each other instead of side-by-side:

```
[noah@linux_lab ~]$ paste -s names.txt lastnames.txt
Alice   Bob     Charlie
Smith   Jones   Brown
```

Examples of paste in Action

Here are a few examples of using paste to combine data:
- **Merging CSV files**: paste -d ',' file1.csv file2.csv > combined.csv
- **Creating a two-column report**: ls -l | paste -d ' ' - - > file_report.txt (the -- tells paste to read from standard input twice)
- **Adding line numbers to a file**: cat file.txt | paste -d ' ' - - > numbered_file.txt (the first - provides line numbers)

The Power of Combination

The paste command, with its ability to merge and align data from multiple sources, is a valuable tool for creating reports, combining datasets, and transforming text into the desired format.

98

4. join – The Data Merger

While `paste` excels at combining data side-by-side, the `join` command takes a more sophisticated approach, merging lines from two files based on a shared key field. It's like a matchmaker for data, bringing together related information from different sources to create a unified view.

Joining on a Common Field

Imagine you have two text files: one containing customer information and another containing order details. Both files share a common field, such as a customer ID. The `join` command allows you to merge these files based on this shared key, creating a combined dataset with information from both sources.

The basic syntax of `join` is:

```
join [options] file1 file2
```

- **file1 and file2**: The two files to be joined.
- **[options]**: Various options to control the join operation, such as specifying the join field, delimiter, and output format.

Join Options – Controlling the Matchmaking

Here are a few key `join` options:
- `-1 field_num`: Specifies the join field number in the first file.
- `-2 field_num`: Specifies the join field number in the second file.
- `-t (delimiter)`: Defines the field delimiter for both input files. The default is whitespace.
- `-o (output format)`: Controls the format of the output, allowing you to specify which fields from each file to include.

An Example of Data Harmony

Let's say you have two files: *customers.txt* and *orders.txt*. The *customers.txt* file has the following format:

```
CustomerID,FirstName,LastName
101,John,Doe
```

```
102,Jane,Smith
103,David,Lee
```

The *orders.txt* file has this format:

```
OrderID,CustomerID,Product
201,101,Laptop
202,103,Keyboard
203,102,Mouse
```

To join these files based on the *CustomerID* field and display the customer name and product ordered:

```
[noah@linux_lab ~]$ join -t ',' -1 1 -2 2 -o 2.2,2.3,1.3 customers.txt
orders.txt
FirstName,LastName,Product
John,Doe,Laptop
Jane,Smith,Mouse
David,Lee,Keyboard
```

This command uses the following options:
- `-t ' , '`: Specifies a comma (,) as the field delimiter.
- `-1 1 -2 2`: Indicates that the join field is the first field in *customers.txt* and the second field in *orders.txt*.
- `-o 2.2,2.3,1.3`: Specifies the output format, including the second and third fields from *orders.txt* and the third field from *customers.txt*.

Joining Forces for Data Insights

The `join` command, with its ability to merge data based on common fields, is a powerful tool for combining information from related sources, creating comprehensive datasets, and gaining deeper insights into your data.

5. Advanced Techniques and Options

Our exploration of `cut`, `paste`, and `join` has revealed their power for basic text manipulation tasks. However, these commands possess a hidden arsenal of advanced techniques and options that can elevate your text processing skills to an even higher level. Let's delve into these hidden gems and unlock their full potential.

cut – Beyond Basic Extraction

- **Multiple Delimiters**: While the `-d` option allows you to specify a single delimiter, you can use the `--output-delimiter` option to define a different delimiter for the output. This is useful when you need to reformat data or convert between different delimiter formats. For example, to convert a tab-delimited file to a comma-separated file:

```
[noah@linux_lab ~]$ cut -f 1-3 --output-delimiter=, data.tsv > data.csv
```

- **Complementing Selections**: The `--complement` option inverts the selection, extracting everything except the specified fields or characters. For example, to remove the first column from a CSV file:

```
[noah@linux_lab ~]$ cut -d ',' -f 2- --complement data.csv
```

paste – Mastering the Merge

- **Serial Merging with -d**: The `-d` option can also be used with `-s` to specify a delimiter between lines when merging files serially. For example, to join lines with a semicolon:

```
[noah@linux_lab ~]$ paste -sd ';' file1.txt file2.txt
```

- **Padding Fields**: The `--delimiters` option allows you to define different delimiters for different fields. This can be helpful for aligning columns or filling in missing data.

join – Advanced Matchmaking

- **Multiple Keys**: You can specify multiple join fields using the `-1` and `-2` options multiple times. For example, `join -1 1 -2 2 -1 3 -2 4 file1.txt file2.txt` would join based on the first and third fields of *file1.txt* and the second and fourth fields of *file2.txt*.

- **Different Join Types**: `join` supports different types of join operations, similar to those found in relational databases:
  - **Inner join (default)**: Outputs only lines where the join field values exist in both files.
  - **Left outer join (-a 1)**: Includes all lines from the first file, even if there's no match in the second file.
  - **Right outer join (-a 2)**: Includes all lines from the second file, even if there's no match in the first file.

Text Processing Power Unleashed

By exploring these advanced techniques and options, you can tackle complex text manipulation tasks with greater precision and flexibility. Remember to consult the `man` pages for each command to discover the full range of possibilities and unleash the true power of your text processing skills.

Chapter Summary

In this chapter, we've transformed into text-processing powerhouses, wielding a formidable trio of commands to extract, combine, and manipulate text data:

- We explored the limitations of basic text tools and the need for more advanced commands to handle structured data and complex text processing tasks.
- We learned how to use `cut` with surgical precision, extracting specific characters or fields from text files and data streams based on delimiters.
- We mastered the art of combining data with `paste`, merging lines from multiple files or columns and aligning fields with different delimiters and options.
- We discovered the power of `join` for merging data based on common fields, creating unified datasets from related sources.
- We delved into advanced techniques and options for each command, unlocking their full potential for complex text manipulation tasks.

Remember, the key to effective text processing often lies in understanding the structure of your data and the role of delimiters. By utilizing the tools and techniques we've covered, you can extract valuable insights, create custom reports, and transform text into the format you desire.

With these skills under your belt, you're well-equipped to tackle a wide range of text processing challenges and continue your journey towards command line mastery.

Chapter 9:
Text Comparison and Patching

Imagine you have two seemingly identical paintings, yet a closer inspection reveals subtle differences in brushstrokes, color palettes, and details. Comparing text files is like examining these paintings, searching for the nuances that distinguish one version from another.

In this chapter, we'll embark on a journey of text comparison and patching, exploring tools that allow you to identify differences between files and apply changes with precision. We'll delve into the commands `comm` and `diff`, learning to decipher their output formats and understand the subtle art of identifying disparities. We'll also explore the concept of patch files – recipes for change – and learn how to apply them using the `patch` command, effectively updating files with the desired modifications. So, grab your metaphorical magnifying glass and prepare to become a text comparison detective!

1. Comparing Text Files – Spotting the Differences

In the ever-changing landscape of data and information, it's often necessary to compare text files and identify the differences between them. Whether you're tracking changes in configuration files, merging code revisions, or simply ensuring the consistency of documents, having the right tools for text comparison is essential.

Why Compare Text Files?

Here are a few common scenarios where text comparison comes in handy:
- **Version Control**: Track changes made to files over time, identify who made the changes, and revert to previous versions if necessary.
- **Software Development**: Compare different versions of source code to identify bugs, analyze changes, and merge code from multiple developers.
- **Configuration Management**: Ensure that configuration files on different systems are consistent and identify any deviations that might cause problems.
- **Data Analysis**: Compare data sets to identify differences, trends, and outliers.
- **Document Revision**: Track changes in documents, such as contracts or manuscripts, and ensure that everyone is working with the latest version.

Tools of the Trade

The Linux command line provides a powerful toolkit for text comparison:
- `comm`: Compares two sorted files line by line, identifying lines that are unique to each file or common to both. It's a simple yet effective tool for basic comparisons.
- `diff`: Offers a more sophisticated approach to text comparison, capable of analyzing files line by line and producing various output formats that describe the changes needed to transform one file into another.

In the following sections, we'll explore these tools in detail and learn how to use them effectively to spot the subtle differences that distinguish one text file from another.

2. comm – Finding Common Ground

The `comm` command is like a diplomatic mediator, helping you find common ground between two sorted text files. It analyzes the files line by line, identifying lines that are unique to each file or shared by both.

Comparing Lines

comm expects two sorted text files as input:

```
comm file1 file2
```

The output of comm is presented in three columns:
- **Column 1**: Lines that are unique to *file1*.
- **Column 2**: Lines that are unique to *file2*.
- **Column 3**: Lines that are common to both files.

For example, let's say you have two files: *list1.txt* and *list2.txt*:

```
[noah@linux_lab ~]$ cat list1.txt
apple
banana
cherry
[noah@linux_lab ~]$ cat list2.txt
banana
cherry
date
```

Comparing these files with comm:

```
[noah@linux_lab ~]$ comm list1.txt list2.txt
apple
                banana
                cherry
        date
```

The output shows that "apple" is unique to *list1.txt*, "date" is unique to *list2.txt*, and both files share the lines "banana" and "cherry".

Controlling the Output

comm offers options to suppress specific columns:
- **-1**: Suppresses the first column (lines unique to *file1*).
- **-2**: Suppresses the second column (lines unique to *file2*).
- **-3**: Suppresses the third column (common lines).

For instance, to display only the lines that are unique to each file:

```
[noah@linux_lab ~]$ comm -3 list1.txt list2.txt
apple
        date
```

Finding Common Ground in Data

`comm` is a valuable tool for comparing lists, configuration files, and other text data where you need to identify commonalities and differences. It's simple yet effective, providing a clear visual representation of how the files relate to each other.

3. diff – A Deeper Dive into Differences

While `comm` provides a basic comparison of lines, the `diff` command delves deeper, analyzing files line by line and generating output that describes the specific changes needed to transform one file into another. It's like having a detective who not only identifies the differences but also provides a detailed report on how to reconcile them.

diff Output Formats

`diff` offers various output formats, each presenting the differences in a unique way:
- **Normal `diff` format**: The default format, which uses cryptic codes to describe the changes needed to convert one file into the other. While concise, it can be difficult to interpret for beginners.
- **Context `diff` format (-c)**: Provides a more readable output, showing the changed lines along with a surrounding context of unchanged lines.
- **Unified `diff` format (-u)**: A more concise version of the context format, displaying only the lines that have changed and a minimal amount of context.

Normal diff Format

The normal `diff` format uses a series of commands to describe changes:
- **a (append)**: Lines need to be appended to the first file.
- **c (change)**: Lines need to be changed in the first file.
- **d (delete)**: Lines need to be deleted from the first file.

Each command is accompanied by line numbers and the actual lines that are affected. While this format is compact, it requires careful interpretation.

107

Context diff Format

The context format, invoked with **-c**, provides a more user-friendly view:

```
[noah@linux_lab ~]$ diff -c list1.txt list2.txt
*** list1.txt      2023-12-09 19:14:30.000000000 -0500
--- list2.txt      2023-12-09 19:15:07.000000000 -0500
***************
*** 1,4 ****
! apple
  banana
  cherry
--- 1,4 ----
  banana
  cherry
! date
```

The output shows the filenames and timestamps, followed by "chunks" of changes. Each chunk begins with line numbers from both files, indicating the range of lines affected. Lines starting with **!** indicate changes, while lines starting with **-** or **+** represent lines removed or added, respectively.

Unified diff Format

The unified format, invoked with **-u**, is similar to the context format but more concise:

```
[noah@linux_lab ~]$ diff -u list1.txt list2.txt
--- list1.txt      2023-12-09 19:14:30.000000000 -0500
+++ list2.txt      2023-12-09 19:15:07.000000000 -0500
@@ -1,4 +1,4 @@
-apple
 banana
 cherry
+date
```

This format displays only the lines that have changed, prefixed with **-** for lines removed and **+** for lines added. The **@@** lines indicate the line numbers and context for each change.

108

Choosing the Right Format

The choice of `diff` format depends on your specific needs and preferences. The normal format is concise but cryptic, while the context and unified formats offer greater readability and are often preferred for analyzing changes and creating patch files.

4. Patch Files – Recipes for Change

The output generated by the `diff` command, particularly in the context or unified format, can be saved as a **patch file**. These patch files act as recipes for change, capturing the differences between two versions of a file and providing instructions on how to transform one version into another.

Capturing Differences

A patch file is essentially a text file containing a series of `diff` commands or change indicators that describe the modifications made to the original file. These modifications might include:
- Lines added to the file.
- Lines removed from the file.
- Lines changed within the file.

The Role of Patch Files

Patch files play a crucial role in software development and version control:
- **Distributing Changes**: Developers often use patch files to share code changes with others. Instead of sending the entire modified file, they can distribute a much smaller patch file that contains only the differences.
- **Updating Software**: Patch files are used to update software by applying bug fixes, security enhancements, or new features.
- **Version Control Systems**: Version control systems like Git use patch files internally to track changes and manage different versions of files.

Patch File Formats

Patch files typically use the context or unified diff format. The header of the patch file contains information about the files involved, such as their names and timestamps.

The body of the patch file contains the diff commands or change indicators that describe the modifications.

Recipes for Transformation

Patch files are like recipes that guide the transformation of one file version into another. In the next section, we'll explore how to use the `patch` command to apply these recipes and update files with the desired changes.

5. patch – Applying the Recipe

The `patch` command is your culinary tool for applying the recipe of changes contained within a patch file. It reads the diff output and modifies the target file accordingly, effectively transforming it into the newer version.

Applying a Patch

To apply a patch, use the following syntax:

```
patch < patch_file
```

This command reads the changes from *patch_file* and applies them to the target file, which is identified by the filename information within the patch file header.

For example, let's say you have a patch file named *changes.patch* that contains modifications for a file called *myfile.txt*. To apply the patch:

```
[noah@linux_lab ~]$ patch < changes.patch
patching file myfile.txt
```

The `patch` command will modify *myfile.txt* according to the instructions in the patch file, effectively updating it to the newer version.

Patch Options

`patch` offers several options to control the patching process:

- **-p num**: Strips a specified number of leading components from file paths mentioned in the patch file. This is useful when the patch file was created with a different directory structure.
- **-E (remove empty files)**: Removes any empty files created as a result of applying the patch.

- **-R (reverse)**: Reverses the patch, effectively undoing the changes.

Patching with Precision

The `patch` command, combined with `diff`, provides a powerful mechanism for managing file changes, updating software, and collaborating on projects. It allows you to distribute and apply changes efficiently and reliably, ensuring that everyone is working with the correct version of files.

6. Applications in Version Control and Software Development

Text comparison and patching play a pivotal role in **version control systems** and **software development**. These systems help developers track changes, collaborate on projects, and manage different versions of source code and other files.

Version Control – A Historical Record

Version control systems, such as Git, Mercurial, and Subversion, maintain a historical record of changes made to files over time. They allow developers to:
- **Track changes**: See who made changes, when they were made, and what modifications were implemented.
- **Revert to previous versions**: Undo mistakes or go back to an earlier version of a file if necessary.
- **Branch and merge**: Create branches for experimental features or bug fixes and then merge them back into the main codebase.
- **Collaborate**: Multiple developers can work on the same project simultaneously, tracking their individual changes and merging them seamlessly.

Diff and Patch in Action

Version control systems heavily utilize `diff` and `patch` behind the scenes:
- `diff` **is used to generate patch files** that capture the differences between file versions. These patch files can be shared with other developers or used to update the software.
- `patch` **is used to apply changes** from patch files, updating files to newer versions or incorporating modifications from other developers.

Software Development Workflow

Here's a typical workflow for using `diff` and `patch` in software development:
1. **A developer makes changes to source code.**
2. **The developer uses `diff` to create a patch file** containing the changes.
3. **The patch file is submitted for review** to other developers or a code repository.
4. **Other developers use `patch` to apply the changes** to their local copies of the code.
5. **The changes are tested and integrated** into the main codebase.

This process ensures that changes are tracked, reviewed, and applied in a controlled and efficient manner, facilitating collaboration and maintaining code quality.

The Power of Collaboration

Text comparison and patching, through tools like `comm`, `diff`, and `patch`, are essential for modern software development and version control, enabling developers to work together effectively, track changes, and manage the evolution of code and other project files.

Chapter Summary

In this chapter, we've donned our detective hats and embarked on a journey of text comparison and patching, uncovering the tools and techniques that allow us to identify and reconcile differences between files:

- We explored the importance of text comparison for tracking changes, managing versions, and ensuring consistency in various applications.
- We learned how to use the `comm` command to compare sorted files and identify lines that are unique or common to each file.
- We delved into the powerful `diff` command and its various output formats (normal, context, unified), learning to decipher the cryptic codes and change indicators to understand file differences.
- We discovered the concept of patch files as recipes for change, capturing the differences between file versions and enabling efficient distribution and application of modifications.
- We mastered the `patch` command, using it to apply changes from patch files and effectively update files to newer versions.

- We explored the crucial role of text comparison and patching in version control systems and software development, understanding how they facilitate collaboration, track changes, and maintain code quality.

Remember, text comparison and patching are essential skills for anyone working with text data, especially in collaborative environments or when managing different versions of files. By utilizing the tools and techniques we've covered, you can become a text comparison expert, identifying and reconciling differences with precision and confidence.

Chapter 10:
The Power of Regular Expressions

Imagine searching for a specific word in a vast library, not by its exact spelling, but by a description of its characteristics – perhaps a word that starts with "s," ends with "e," and has two vowels in between. **Regular expressions**, often abbreviated as **regex**, provide a similar ability to describe and match patterns in text, turning you into a master word detective.

In this chapter, we'll unlock the power of regex, exploring its unique language of metacharacters, anchors, and quantifiers. You'll learn to craft expressions that match complex patterns, enabling you to search, filter, and manipulate text data with precision and efficiency. Get ready to embark on a journey into the world of pattern matching and discover the versatility and power of regular expressions!

1. Regular Expressions – The Pattern Matching Language

Regular expressions, often referred to as **regex** or **regexp**, are a specialized language for describing patterns in text. They provide a concise and flexible way to match, locate, and manage text, making them an invaluable tool for a wide range of tasks.

The Power of Patterns

Imagine you're tasked with finding all email addresses within a large document. Searching for each individual email address would be tedious and time-consuming. However, with regex, you can define a pattern that describes the general structure of an email address – a series of characters followed by an "@" symbol, followed by a domain name – and let the computer do the searching for you.

This ability to describe patterns is what makes regex so powerful. Instead of searching for exact matches, you can define criteria that encompass a wide range of possibilities, allowing you to:

- **Search for specific words or phrases**: Find all occurrences of a particular word or phrase within a text file or data stream.
- **Identify patterns**: Match phone numbers, email addresses, URLs, or any other textual pattern that follows a predictable structure.
- **Validate data**: Ensure that input data conforms to a specific format, such as a date, a social security number, or a credit card number.
- **Extract information**: Isolate and extract specific parts of text based on patterns, such as usernames, file extensions, or numerical values.
- **Modify text**: Perform search and replace operations, changing text based on patterns.

Applications of Regex

Regex is widely used in various domains:

- **Text editors**: Search and replace functionality often relies on regex for pattern matching.
- **Programming languages**: Many programming languages, such as Python, Perl, and JavaScript, have built-in support for regex, allowing developers to process and manipulate text data.

- **Command-line tools**: Numerous command-line tools, including `grep`, `sed` (we will see it in more detail in the next chapter), and `awk`, utilize regex for searching, filtering, and transforming text.

A Versatile Language

Regex is a versatile language that can be applied to a wide range of text processing challenges. By learning the fundamentals of regex, you'll unlock a powerful tool for efficiently finding, manipulating, and understanding textual information.

2. Building Blocks of Regex – Literals and Metacharacters

Regular expressions are constructed using a combination of literal characters and metacharacters, like building a structure with bricks and mortar. Literal characters represent themselves, while metacharacters act as special symbols with specific meanings for defining patterns.

Literal Characters – Building the Foundation

Literal characters in regex match themselves exactly. For example, the regex "cat" would match the word "cat" and only the word "cat". Any alphanumeric character or symbol can be used as a literal character.

Metacharacters – The Special Symbols

Metacharacters are the mortar that holds the regex structure together, providing special meanings and functionalities:
- **. (dot)**: Matches any single character except a newline. For example, the regex "c.t" would match "cat", "cut", "cbt", or any other three-letter word starting with "c" and ending with "t".
- *** (asterisk)**: Matches zero or more repetitions of the preceding character. For example, the regex "ca*t" would match "ct", "cat", "caat", "caaat", or any other string starting with "c" and ending with "t" with any number of "a"s in between.
- **+ (plus)**: Matches one or more repetitions of the preceding character. For example, "ca+t" would match "cat", "caat", "caaat", but not "ct".
- **? (question mark)**: Matches zero or one occurrence of the preceding character. For example, "colou?r" would match both "color" and "colour".

- **[ ] (square brackets)**: Defines a character class, matching any single character within the brackets. For example, "[aeiou]" would match any vowel, and "[0-9]" would match any digit.

Combining the Building Blocks

By combining literal characters and metacharacters, you can build complex patterns to match specific sequences of characters, words, or formats. For example, the regex "[A-Za-z0-9]+" would match one or more alphanumeric characters, and the regex "https?://[^\s]+" would match a URL starting with either "http://" or "https://" followed by one or more non-whitespace characters.

Understanding the roles of literal characters and metacharacters is the first step towards mastering the art of building regular expressions.

3. Anchors – Marking the Boundaries

While literal characters and metacharacters define the building blocks of regular expressions, **anchors** act as markers that define specific positions within the text, ensuring that matches occur only at the designated locations. They are like the cornerstones of a building, providing stability and structure to the regex pattern.

The Power of ^ and $

There are two primary anchors in regex:
- ^ **(caret)**: Matches the beginning of a line. For example, the regex "^cat" would only match lines that start with the word "cat".
- $ **(dollar sign)**: Matches the end of a line. For example, the regex "dog$" would only match lines that end with the word "dog".

Anchoring for Precision

Anchors are essential for ensuring that your regex matches occur at the desired positions within the text. Here are a few examples of using anchors for precise matching:
- **Matching lines starting with a specific word**: `^Error:` would match lines that begin with the word "Error:" followed by any characters.
- **Matching lines ending with a number**: `[0-9]$` would match lines that end with a single digit.
- **Matching entire lines**: `^...$` would match lines that contain exactly three characters.

Anchoring in Action

Here are some examples of using anchors with the `grep` command:
- **Find lines starting with "WARNING"**: `grep "^WARNING" logfile.txt`
- **Find lines ending with a colon (:)**: `grep ":$" config.txt`
- **Find blank lines**: `grep "^$" myfile.txt`

Marking the Territory

Anchors, in conjunction with other regex elements, allow you to define precise patterns and ensure that your matches occur only at the intended locations within the text, providing greater control and accuracy in your text processing tasks.

4. Character Classes – Matching Sets of Characters

While individual characters and metacharacters allow you to match specific elements, **character classes** provide a way to match any character from a defined set. They are like buckets filled with characters, allowing you to specify a category of characters that should be matched at a particular position in the regex pattern.

Predefined Character Classes

Regex offers several predefined character classes for common sets of characters:
- **[:alnum:]**: Matches any alphanumeric character (letters and numbers).
- **[:alpha:]**: Matches any alphabetic character (letters only).
- **[:digit:]**: Matches any digit (0-9).
- **[:lower:]**: Matches any lowercase letter.
- **[:upper:]**: Matches any uppercase letter.
- **[:space:]**: Matches whitespace characters (spaces, tabs, newlines).
- **[:punct:]**: Matches punctuation characters.

Building Your Own Character Classes

You can create custom character classes by enclosing a set of characters within square brackets [ ]. For example:
- **[aeiou]**: Matches any vowel.
- **[0-9a-fA-F]**: Matches any hexadecimal digit.
- **[,.!?]**: Matches common punctuation marks.

Negated Character Classes

You can also define negated character classes by placing a caret (^) as the first character within the brackets. This matches any character that is **not** in the set. For example:
- **[^0-9]**: Matches any character that is not a digit.
- **[^aeiou]**: Matches any character that is not a vowel.

Examples of Character Classes

Here are some examples of using character classes with `grep`:
- **Find lines containing words starting with a vowel**: `grep "^[aeiou][[:alpha:]]*" words.txt`
- **Find lines containing hexadecimal numbers**: `grep "[[:xdigit:]]+" data.txt`
- **Find lines that don't start with a number**: `grep "^[^[:digit:]]" data.txt`

Categorizing Characters

Character classes provide a powerful way to categorize and match sets of characters, expanding the versatility and expressiveness of your regular expressions.

5. Quantifiers – Specifying Repetitions

Imagine a recipe that calls for "a handful of blueberries" – the exact quantity is flexible, but there's a general range. **Quantifiers** in regular expressions provide a similar ability to specify the number of times a character or group should be matched, adding flexibility and expressiveness to your patterns.

Quantifier Symbols

Regex offers several quantifiers, each with a specific meaning:
- *** (asterisk)**: Matches zero or more repetitions of the preceding character or group. For example, "ca*t" matches "ct" (zero "a"s), "cat" (one "a"), "caat" (two "a"s), and so on.
- **+ (plus)**: Matches one or more repetitions of the preceding character or group. For example, "ca+t" matches "cat", "caat", "caaat", but not "ct".
- **? (question mark)**: Matches zero or one occurrence of the preceding character or group. For example, "colou?r" matches both "color" and "colour".

- **{n}**: Matches exactly n repetitions of the preceding character or group. For example, "a{3}" matches "aaa" but not "aa" or "aaaa".
- **{n,m}**: Matches between n and m repetitions (inclusive) of the preceding character or group. For example, "a{2,4}" matches "aa", "aaa", or "aaaa", but not "a" or "aaaaa".
- **{n,}**: Matches at least n repetitions of the preceding character or group. For example, "a{2,}" matches "aa", "aaa", "aaaa", and so on.

Examples of Quantifier Usage

Here are some examples of using quantifiers with `grep`:
- **Find lines with words containing three or more vowels**: `grep "[aeiou]{3,}" words.txt`
- **Find lines with at least two consecutive digits**: `grep "[0-9]{2,}" data.txt`
- **Find lines starting with "Error" followed by any number of spaces**: `grep "^Error *" logfile.txt`

The Power of Flexibility

Quantifiers allow you to define patterns with varying degrees of repetition, making your regex expressions more flexible and adaptable to different scenarios. By mastering the art of using quantifiers, you can create patterns that match a wider range of possibilities and extract more precise information from your text data.

6. Basic vs. Extended Regular Expressions

As you delve deeper into the world of regular expressions, you'll encounter two main flavors: **basic regular expressions (BRE)** and **extended regular expressions (ERE)**. While both share the fundamental principles of pattern matching, they differ in their syntax and the range of metacharacters they support.

BRE – The Traditional Foundation

Basic regular expressions are the older and more traditional form of regex, adhering to the original specifications of early Unix tools. BRE recognizes a limited set of metacharacters, including: ., *, [ ], ^, and $

To use the additional metacharacters available in ERE within BRE, you need to escape them with a backslash (\): \?, \+, \|, \(\), and \{ \}

ERE – Extended Power and Flexibility

Extended regular expressions build upon the foundation of BRE, offering a richer set of metacharacters and greater flexibility in pattern matching:
- All BRE metacharacters are recognized without escaping.
- Additional metacharacters include:
  - ?
  - +
  - | (alternation)
  - ( ) (grouping)
  - { } (interval quantifiers)

Choosing the Right Flavor

The choice between BRE and ERE often depends on the tools you're using and your personal preference. Many older Unix utilities, such as `grep` and `sed`, default to BRE, while newer tools and programming languages often support ERE by default.

Here's a table summarizing the key differences:

Metacharacter	BRE	ERE
?	\?	?
+	\+	+
()	\(\)	()
{}	\{\}	{}

Regex Evolution

As you become more proficient with regular expressions, you'll appreciate the additional power and flexibility offered by ERE. However, it's important to be aware of the differences between BRE and ERE, especially when working with older tools or scripts that might still rely on the basic syntax.

7. Regex in Action – Command-Line Applications

Regular expressions are not just theoretical constructs; they are powerful tools that can be applied to a wide range of tasks on the Linux command line. Let's explore how regex enhances the capabilities of various command-line tools, turning them into versatile instruments for text processing and data manipulation.

grep – Searching with Regex Precision

The `grep` command, as we saw in Chapter 7, is a master text searcher, and regular expressions provide the ability to define precise search patterns. Here are a few examples:

- Find lines containing email addresses: `grep '[^@]+@[^@]+\.[^@]+' email_list.txt`
- Find lines starting with "Error" or "Warning": `grep -E '^(Error|Warning)' logfile.txt`
- Find lines with words containing at least three consecutive consonants: `grep '[^aeiou]{3}' words.txt`

sed – Transforming Text with Regex

The `sed` stream editor, as we will explore in Chapter 11, becomes even more powerful when combined with regex. Here are some examples:

- Replace all occurrences of "color" or "colour" with "colour": `sed 's/colou?r/colour/g' textfile.txt`
- Delete lines containing IP addresses: `sed '/[0-9]{1,3}\.[0-9]{1,3}\.[0-9]{1,3}\.[0-9]{1,3}/d' logfile.txt`
- Extract the first word from each line: `sed 's/\([^ ]*\).*/\1/' data.txt`

awk – Processing Data with Regex Patterns

The `awk` command is a versatile tool for data extraction and processing, and regex enhances its pattern matching capabilities:

- Print lines where the second field is a number: `awk '$2 ~ /^[0-9]+$/' data.txt`
- Extract email addresses and usernames: `awk -F ':' '/^[^@]+@[^@]+\.[^@]+$/ {print $1}' email_list.txt`

Regex – A Universal Language

These examples demonstrate the versatility of regular expressions across different command-line tools. Regex is a universal language for pattern matching, empowering you to search, filter, and manipulate text data with precision and efficiency.

Chapter Summary

In this chapter, we've delved into the powerful world of regular expressions, unlocking a versatile language for describing and matching patterns in text:

- We explored the concept of regular expressions and their applications in various contexts, from text editors to programming languages and command-line tools.
- We learned about the building blocks of regex – literal characters and metacharacters – and their roles in constructing patterns.
- We explored commonly used metacharacters, such as ., *, +, ?, and [ ], and learned how to use them to match specific characters, sequences, and patterns.
- We discovered the importance of anchors (^ and $) for matching the beginning and end of lines, ensuring precise pattern placement.
- We explored character classes, both predefined and custom, for matching sets of characters and categories.
- We learned how to use quantifiers to specify the number of repetitions, adding flexibility and expressiveness to our regex patterns.
- We discussed the difference between basic and extended regular expressions, understanding the additional metacharacters and capabilities offered by ERE.
- We witnessed regex in action, exploring its application with command-line tools like `grep`, `sed`, and `awk`.

Regular expressions are a powerful and essential skill for any aspiring command line user. By mastering the art of pattern matching, you can efficiently search, filter, and manipulate text data, unlocking new levels of productivity and insight.

With a solid understanding of regex under your belt, you're now well-prepared to tackle the next chapter and explore the advanced text editing capabilities of the `sed` command, where regex will play a crucial role in performing intricate text transformations.

Chapter 11:
Advanced Text Editing with sed

Imagine having a robot assistant who can meticulously edit and transform text files according to your instructions, without requiring you to lift a finger. The **sed** command, short for "stream editor," is that robotic assistant, a powerful tool for non-interactive text manipulation.

sed operates like a skilled surgeon, working its magic on streams of text, applying changes line by line with precision and efficiency. In this chapter, we'll explore the inner workings of **sed**, learning its language of commands and addresses, and wielding the power of regular expressions to perform intricate text transformations. Prepare to unlock the full potential of **sed** and become a master of automated text editing!

1. sed – The Stream Editor

The `sed` command, a stalwart of the Unix tradition and a cornerstone of text processing in Linux, stands for "stream editor." Unlike interactive text editors like `vim` or `nano` where you manually navigate and modify text, `sed` operates on streams of text, applying edits automatically based on specified commands and patterns.

Editing in the Flow

`sed` works its magic by reading input from a file or standard input, processing each line of text individually, and then outputting the modified text to standard output. This stream-oriented approach makes `sed` ideal for:

- **Automation**: You can create scripts containing `sed` commands to automate repetitive editing tasks, saving time and effort.
- **Batch Processing**: `sed` can efficiently process large numbers of files, applying edits to each file in a consistent manner.
- **Non-Interactive Editing**: `sed` is perfect for situations where interactive editing is impractical or undesirable, such as in scripts or when working with remote systems.

The Power of sed

Here are a few examples of what you can accomplish with `sed`:

- **Search and replace**: Replace specific words or patterns of text throughout a file or data stream.
- **Delete lines**: Remove lines based on patterns or line numbers.
- **Insert text**: Add new lines or text at specific locations within a file.
- **Transform data**: Modify the format or structure of text, such as converting delimiters or extracting specific fields.

A Non-Interactive Powerhouse

While `sed` might seem enigmatic at first, its non-interactive nature and powerful editing capabilities make it an invaluable tool for text processing tasks. In the following sections, we'll unravel the mysteries of `sed` commands and addresses, and unleash the full potential of this versatile text editor.

2. sed Commands – The Editing Toolkit

The `sed` command offers a versatile toolkit of editing operations, allowing you to perform a wide range of text manipulations. Each `sed` command is like a specialized tool, designed for a specific editing task.

The Structure of sed Commands

`sed` commands follow a basic structure:

```
[address]command[options]
```

- **[address] (optional)**: Specifies the line or lines on which the command should operate. If no address is specified, the command is applied to every line of the input.
- **command**: The editing operation to perform, such as substitution, deletion, or printing.
- **[options] (optional)**: Modifiers that affect the behavior of the command.

Common sed Commands

Here are a few essential sed commands and their functions:
- **s (substitute)**: The workhorse of `sed`, the s command replaces text based on patterns. It uses the following syntax:

```
s/pattern/replacement/flags
```

-     ○ **pattern**: A regular expression or fixed string defining the text to be replaced.
-     ○ **replacement**: The new text to substitute for the matched pattern.
-     ○ **flags (optional)**: Modifiers that control the substitution behavior, such as **g** (global) to replace all occurrences on a line, or **i** (ignore case) to perform a case-insensitive search.
- **d (delete)**: Removes lines that match the specified address. For example, **2d** would delete the second line, and **/error/d** would delete any lines containing the word "error".
- **p (print)**: Prints lines that match the specified address. By default, `sed` prints all lines, so the **p** command is often used with the **-n** option to suppress automatic printing and selectively display specific lines.
- **a (append)**: Adds new lines of text after the lines matching the address.

- i **(insert)**: Inserts new lines of text before the lines matching the address.
- c **(change)**: Replaces the lines matching the address with the specified new text.

Building Your Editing Skills

These basic `sed` commands provide a foundation for performing a wide range of text manipulations. In the following sections, we'll explore how to use addresses to target specific lines, unleash the power of regular expressions for pattern matching, and discover options for fine-tuning the behavior of `sed`.

3. Addresses – Targeting the Text

Imagine an archer aiming at a specific target on an archery range. Similarly, `sed` commands require precise targeting to ensure they act upon the correct lines of text. Addresses provide this targeting mechanism, specifying which lines in the input stream should be affected by a particular command.

Addressing Modes

`sed` offers various ways to address lines:
- **Line numbers**: You can specify a single line number (e.g., `1`, `5`) or a range of line numbers (e.g., `1,5`) to target specific lines. For example, `3d` would delete the third line, and `2,4p` would print lines 2 through 4.
- **Regular expressions**: Use a regular expression enclosed in slashes (e.g., `/pattern/`) to address lines that match the pattern. For example, `/error/d` would delete any lines containing the word "error", and `s/old/new/g` would replace all occurrences of "old" with "new" on every line.
- **Step increments**: You can specify a starting line and a step increment using the tilde (~) operator to address lines at regular intervals. For example, `1~2` would address every other line starting from the first line, and `5~5` would address every fifth line starting from the fifth line.

Examples of Address Targeting

Here are a few examples of using addresses to target specific lines:
- **Delete the first line**: `1d`
- **Print lines 5 to 10**: `5,10p`
- **Replace "old" with "new" on lines containing "error"**: `/error/s/old/new/g`
- **Insert a comment at the beginning of the file**: `1i\# This is a comment`
- **Append a blank line after every fifth line**: `1~5a\`

Sharpening Your Aim

Addresses are essential for directing sed commands to the correct targets, allowing for precise and efficient text manipulation. By understanding the different addressing modes and how to combine them with editing commands, you gain greater control over the editing process and can achieve intricate text transformations.

4. Regular Expressions with sed – The Power of Patterns

While basic sed commands provide a foundation for text editing, the true power of sed is unleashed when combined with **regular expressions (regex)**. Regex allows you to define complex patterns for matching and manipulating text, transforming sed into a precision instrument for intricate text surgery.

Regex – A Quick Recap

Recall from Chapter 10 that regular expressions are a symbolic language for describing patterns in text. They use a combination of literal characters and metacharacters to match specific sequences of characters, words, or patterns. Here's a quick refresher on some common regex elements:

- **Literal characters**: Match themselves (e.g., "a", "b", "1", "2").
- **Metacharacters**:
    - . (dot): Matches any single character.
    - * (asterisk): Matches zero or more repetitions of the preceding character.
    - + (plus): Matches one or more repetitions of the preceding character.
    - ? (question mark): Matches zero or one occurrence of the preceding character.
    - [] (square brackets): Matches any single character within the brackets.
    - ^ (caret): Matches the beginning of a line.
    - $ (dollar sign): Matches the end of a line.
- **Character classes**: Predefined sets of characters (e.g., [:alnum:], [:digit:]).

Regex with the s Command

The **s** (substitute) command is where regular expressions truly shine in sed. It allows you to search for complex patterns and replace them with new text. For example, to replace all occurrences of email addresses with the word "REDACTED":

```
sed 's/[^@]+@[^@]+\.[^@]+/REDACTED/g' email_list.txt
```

This command uses the following regex: [^@]+@[^@]+\.[^@]+, which matches any sequence of characters that:

1. Does not contain an "@" symbol ([^@]+).
2. Is followed by an "@" symbol.
3. Is followed by another sequence of characters that does not contain an "@" symbol.
4. Is followed by a dot (.).
5. Ends with a sequence of characters that does not contain an "@" symbol.

Examples of Regex Power

Here are a few more examples of using regex with `sed`:

- **Replace all phone numbers with "XXX-XXX-XXXX"**: `sed 's/([0-9]{3})-[0-9]{3}-[0-9]{4}/XXX-XXX-XXXX/g' phone_list.txt`
- **Remove all HTML tags**: `sed 's/<[^>]*>//g' html_file.html`
- **Extract the second word from each line**: `sed 's/^[^ ]* \([^ ]*\).*/\1/' textfile.txt`

Mastering the Art of Pattern Matching

By combining `sed` with the power of regular expressions, you can perform intricate text transformations and data manipulations with surgical precision. As you explore the possibilities of regex, you'll discover a world of creative solutions for complex text processing challenges.

5. sed Options – Fine-Tuning the Editor

While `sed` commands and addresses provide the core functionality for text manipulation, a set of options act as fine-tuning knobs, allowing you to control the behavior of `sed` and customize its output.

Essential sed Options

Here are a few essential `sed` options:

- **-i (in-place)**: By default, `sed` sends its edited output to standard output. The `-i` option instructs `sed` to modify the input files directly, making changes "in-place" without creating a separate output file. For example, to replace all occurrences of "old" with "new" in a file named *myfile.txt*:

```
[noah@linux_lab ~]$ sed -i 's/old/new/g' myfile.txt
```

- -n **(quiet)**: Normally, sed prints every line of the input after processing it. The -n option suppresses this automatic printing, allowing you to use the p command to selectively print specific lines. This is useful for extracting specific information or creating more controlled output. For example, to print only lines containing the word "error":

```
[noah@linux_lab ~]$ sed -n '/error/p' logfile.txt
```

- -e **(expression)**: Allows you to specify multiple editing commands on the command line. This is useful for performing a series of edits in one go. For example, to delete the first line and replace "old" with "new" on all other lines:

```
[noah@linux_lab ~]$ sed -e '1d' -e 's/old/new/g' myfile.txt
```

- -f **(file)**: Reads editing commands from a script file, allowing you to create reusable scripts for complex text processing tasks. We'll explore sed scripts in the next section.

Fine-Tuning for Precision

These options provide additional control and flexibility, allowing you to tailor the behavior of sed to your specific needs. By understanding and utilizing these options effectively, you can achieve more precise and efficient text editing results.

6. sed Scripts – Automating Transformations

While sed commands can be executed individually on the command line, complex text processing tasks often require a series of coordinated edits. **sed scripts** provide a way to automate these transformations, allowing you to create reusable recipes for text manipulation.

Scripting with sed

A sed script is simply a text file containing one or more sed commands, each on a separate line. You can then execute the script using the -f option:

```
sed -f script_file input_file
```

This command reads the editing commands from *script_file* and applies them to the contents of *input_file*, sending the modified output to standard output.

Building a Script

Let's create a simple `sed` script to demonstrate the process. We'll write a script named *format.sed* that performs the following tasks:
1. Deletes the first line.
2. Converts all text to uppercase.
3. Replaces spaces with underscores.

```
1d
y/abcdefghijklmnopqrstuvwxyz/ABCDEFGHIJKLMNOPQRSTUVWXYZ/
s/ /_/g
```

To execute this script on a file named *data.txt*:

```
[noah@linux_lab ~]$ sed -f format.sed data.txt
```

Scripting for Complex Tasks

`sed` scripts are powerful tools for automating complex text processing tasks, such as:
- **Data cleaning**: Removing unwanted characters, correcting formatting errors, and standardizing data formats.
- **File conversion**: Converting between different file formats, such as CSV to tab-delimited or vice versa.
- **Report generation**: Extracting and formatting data to create reports or summaries.
- **Text transformation**: Performing complex search and replace operations, manipulating text structure, or applying custom formatting.

Automation and Reusability

By creating `sed` scripts, you can automate repetitive editing tasks and build a library of reusable text processing tools. This saves time and effort, improves consistency, and allows you to tackle complex text manipulation challenges with ease.

131

Chapter Summary

In this chapter, we've journeyed into the depths of the sed stream editor, unlocking its power for advanced text manipulation and automation:

- We learned how sed operates as a non-interactive text editor, processing text streams line by line and applying edits automatically.
- We explored the essential sed commands, including s for substitution, d for deletion, p for printing, and commands for inserting and changing text.
- We mastered the art of targeting specific lines with addresses, using line numbers, regular expressions, and step increments to direct our editing commands.
- We combined the power of sed with regular expressions, enabling complex pattern matching and intricate text transformations.
- We explored options like -i for in-place editing and -n for controlling output, fine-tuning the behavior of sed to suit our needs.
- We learned to create sed scripts, automating complex text processing tasks and building reusable tools for efficient text manipulation.

The sed command is a powerful and versatile tool for anyone who works with text data. By mastering its commands, addresses, options, and scripting capabilities, you can perform a wide range of text processing tasks with precision and efficiency, saving time and effort and unlocking new levels of command line mastery.

Part 3: Bash Scripting and Automation

Chapter 12:
Writing Your First Script

Imagine having the ability to capture the magic of the command line and encapsulate it into reusable spells. That, my friend, is the essence of **shell scripting**. Shell scripts are like enchanted scrolls, containing a series of commands that the shell can execute as a single unit, automating tasks and saving you from repetitive typing.

In this chapter, we'll embark on our journey as scriptwriters, crafting our very first shell script. We'll explore the structure of a script, learn how to imbue it with executable powers, and discover the `echo` command – our script's voice to the outside world. So, prepare to unleash your inner sorcerer and begin your adventure into the enchanting realm of shell scripting!

1. Shell Scripting – Automating the Command Line

The Linux command line, with its vast array of tools and utilities, offers immense power and flexibility. However, performing repetitive tasks or complex sequences of commands can become tedious and time-consuming. This is where **shell scripting** comes to the rescue, providing a way to automate these tasks and unleash the true potential of the command line.

Shell Scripts – Your Automation Spells

A shell script is essentially a plain text file containing a series of commands that the shell can execute as a single unit. It's like a recipe for the command line, listing the ingredients and instructions for a specific task. By creating scripts, you can:

- **Automate repetitive tasks**: Instead of typing the same sequence of commands over and over again, you can capture them in a script and execute it with a single command.
- **Improve efficiency**: Scripts save you time and effort by automating tasks, allowing you to focus on more complex or creative endeavors.
- **Increase accuracy**: Scripts reduce the risk of human error by ensuring that commands are executed consistently and in the correct order.
- **Build complex workflows**: You can combine multiple commands and logic within a script to create sophisticated workflows for data processing, system administration, and other tasks.
- **Share and collaborate**: Scripts can be easily shared with others, allowing for collaboration and knowledge sharing.

The Shell as Interpreter

Shell scripts are interpreted by the shell, which means that the shell reads and executes each command line by line. This differs from compiled programs, which are translated into machine code before execution. The advantage of interpreted scripts is that they are easier to write and modify, making them ideal for rapid prototyping and experimentation.

Unleashing the Power of Automation

Shell scripting is a valuable skill for any Linux user, from beginners seeking to simplify routine tasks to experienced system administrators and developers building complex automation tools. In the following sections, we'll embark on our scripting journey by creating our first script and exploring the fundamental elements of shell scripting.

2. Crafting Your First Script

With the power of shell scripting at our fingertips, let's embark on the exciting journey of creating our very first script. We'll begin with a classic – the "Hello, World!" program – a simple yet profound introduction to the world of scripting.

Creating the Script File

1. **Choose a Text Editor**: You can use any text editor you're comfortable with, such as `vim`, `nano`, or `gedit`. The choice of editor is a matter of personal preference, but it's helpful to use one that supports syntax highlighting for shell scripts, which can improve readability and help you spot errors.
2. **Create a New File**: Create a new file and name it *hello_world.sh*. The `.sh` extension is a common convention for shell scripts, but it's not strictly required.

Script Structure

- **Shebang Line**: The first line of your script should be the shebang line:

```
#!/bin/bash
```

The shebang line tells the system which interpreter to use to execute the script. In this case, we're specifying the Bash shell (/bin/bash) as the interpreter.

- **Comments**: Comments are lines that begin with a hash symbol (#). They are ignored by the shell and serve to document your code, explain its purpose, and provide clarity for yourself and others who might read the script.

```
# This is a comment
# This script displays a greeting message.
```

- **Commands**: The remaining lines of your script will contain the actual commands you want to execute.

Adding the Greeting

For our "Hello, World!" script, we'll use the `echo` command to display the message:

138

```
echo "Hello, World!"
```

The Complete Script

Here's the complete *hello_world.sh* script:

```
#!/bin/bash
# This script displays a greeting message.
echo "Hello, World!"
```

Save this script file and prepare to make it executable in the next step.

3. Making it Executable – Granting Script Powers

Our *hello_world.sh* script is complete, but it's currently just a plain text file. To empower it to run as a program, we need to grant it **executable** permissions.

chmod to the Rescue

The `chmod` command, as we learned in Chapter 6, is our tool for modifying file permissions. To make our script executable, we'll use the following syntax:

```
chmod +x script_file
```

The `+x` option adds execute permission for the owner, group, and others. Applying this to our script:

```
[noah@linux_lab ~]$ chmod +x hello_world.sh
```

Permission Options

You have several options when setting execute permissions:
- `+x`: Grants execute permission to all users (owner, group, and others). This is suitable for scripts that you want anyone on the system to be able to run.
- `u+x`: Grants execute permission only to the owner. This is appropriate for personal scripts that you don't want others to execute.
- `g+x`: Grants execute permission to the group owner. This can be useful for scripts that are shared among a group of users.

Verifying Executable Status

You can verify the permissions of your script using ls -l:

```
[noah@linux_lab ~]$ ls -l hello_world.sh
-rwxr-xr-x 1 noah noah 72 Dec 10 10:22 hello_world.sh
```

The x in the permission string indicates that the file is executable.

With execute permissions granted, our script is now empowered to run as a program.

4. Running Your Script

Now that your script has execute permission, you can run it in several ways:
- **Using the full path:**

```
[noah@linux_lab ~]$ /home/noah/hello_world.sh
```

This method specifies the absolute path to the script, ensuring the shell can locate and execute it regardless of your current directory or PATH environment variable.
- **Using a relative path:**

```
[noah@linux_lab ~]$ ./hello_world.sh
```

If the script is in your current working directory, you can use ./ followed by the script name. The ./ tells the shell to look for the script in the current directory.
- **Using the script name directly (if in PATH):**

```
[noah@linux_lab ~]$ hello_world.sh
```

If you've placed the script in a directory listed in your PATH environment variable (e.g., ~/bin), you can execute it by simply typing its name at the prompt.

Choosing the Execution Method

The most convenient way to run your script depends on its location and your workflow. Using the full path is always reliable, while using the script name directly is the most convenient if it's in your PATH.

5. Where to Place Your Script – Choosing a Home

Our script is now executable, but where should we put it? Choosing the right location for your scripts is important for both organization and ease of execution.

Script File Naming

- **Descriptive Names**: Use clear and descriptive names that reflect the purpose of the script. This makes it easier to identify and remember what the script does. For example, a script that backs up your home directory could be named *backup_home.sh*.
- **Avoid Spaces**: It's generally best to avoid spaces in script filenames, as they can cause issues with command-line parsing. Use underscores (_) or hyphens (-) to separate words if needed.

Script Locations

- `~/bin` **directory**: Most Linux distributions include a `bin` directory within your home directory and automatically add it to your PATH environment variable. This makes it a convenient location for storing personal scripts that you want to be able to execute from anywhere.
- `/usr/local/bin`: This directory is a traditional location for locally installed software, including scripts that are intended for use by all users on the system. However, you'll typically need superuser privileges to place scripts in this directory.
- **Project-specific directories**: If you're working on a specific project, you might create a dedicated directory for scripts related to that project.

The PATH to Execution

The PATH environment variable, as we discussed in Chapter 4, contains a colon-separated list of directories where the shell searches for executable programs. When you type a command at the prompt, the shell looks for it in these directories.

```
[noah@linux_lab ~]$ echo $PATH
/home/noah/bin:/usr/local/bin:/usr/bin:/bin
```

Placing your script in one of the directories listed in your PATH ensures that you can execute it by simply typing its name at the prompt, without having to specify the full path each time.

Choosing the Right Home

The best location for your script depends on its purpose and intended audience. For personal scripts, `~/bin` is a convenient and accessible choice. For scripts shared with other users or intended for system-wide use, `/usr/local/bin` or a project-specific directory might be more appropriate.

By choosing a suitable location and giving your script a clear and descriptive name, you ensure that it's well-organized and easy to find and execute.

6. echo – Speaking from the Script

Our script is now executable and has a suitable home within the file system. But how does it communicate with the outside world? The `echo` command acts as the voice of your script, allowing you to display messages, output data, and provide feedback to the user.

Printing Text with echo

The `echo` command is simple yet powerful. It prints its arguments to standard output, displaying them on the terminal screen. For example, to display the message "Hello from the script":

```
echo "Hello from the script"
```

You can use double quotes or single quotes to enclose the text, and you can include variables or command substitutions within the string:

```
message="Greetings, $USER!"
echo "$message"

current_date=$(date)
echo "Today's date is: $current_date"
```

Controlling Newlines

By default, `echo` adds a newline character at the end of its output, causing the cursor to move to the beginning of the next line. To suppress this newline, use the `-n` option:

```
echo -n "Enter your name: "
read name
echo "Welcome, $name!"
```

This script demonstrates using `echo -n` to display a prompt without a newline, allowing the user to enter their name on the same line.

Formatting Output

`echo` also supports escape sequences for formatting output:
- `\n`: Newline character.
- `\t`: Tab character.

For more advanced formatting options, consider using the `printf` command, which we'll explore in later chapters.

Giving Your Script a Voice

The `echo` command is your script's primary means of communication, allowing you to display messages, output data, and provide feedback to the user. By mastering the use of `echo`, you give your scripts a voice and make them more interactive and informative.

Chapter Summary

In this chapter, we've embarked on our journey as scriptwriters, creating and executing our first shell script and exploring the fundamental elements of shell scripting:
- We introduced the concept of shell scripting as a way to automate command-line tasks, improving efficiency, accuracy, and repeatability.
- We guided you through creating a simple "Hello, World!" script, understanding the basic structure of a script file and the role of the shebang line and comments.
- We learned how to make a script executable using the `chmod` command, granting it the power to run as a program.
- We discussed best practices for script file naming and location, exploring options like the `~/bin` directory and the importance of the PATH environment variable.
- We introduced the `echo` command as the voice of your scripts, allowing you to display messages, output data, and provide feedback to the user.

Remember, shell scripting is a valuable skill that can save you time and effort, automate repetitive tasks, and unlock new levels of command-line mastery. As you continue your journey, you'll build upon these foundational concepts and explore more advanced scripting techniques, creating powerful tools and automating your workflow with the magic of shell scripts.

In the next chapter, we'll delve into the building blocks of scripting, exploring variables, constants, and various methods for assigning values, setting the stage for more complex and dynamic scripts.

Chapter 13:
Scripting Building Blocks

Imagine constructing a building – you need bricks, mortar, beams, and various materials to create a sturdy and functional structure. Similarly, shell scripts rely on fundamental building blocks to store data, perform calculations, and control the flow of execution.

In this chapter, we'll explore these essential building blocks – **variables** and **constants** – and learn how to use them effectively to create dynamic and powerful scripts. We'll discover different ways to assign values, unleash the magic of expansions to manipulate data, and explore techniques for embedding blocks of text within our scripts. So, grab your metaphorical toolbox and prepare to lay the foundation for your scripting masterpieces!

1. Variables – The Data Containers

Variables in shell scripts are like containers that hold data, allowing you to store information, perform operations on it, and reference it throughout your script. They are essential for creating dynamic and flexible scripts that can adapt to different inputs and conditions.

Naming Your Containers

Variable names in Bash follow these rules:
- **Start with a letter or underscore**: The first character of a variable name must be a letter (a-z, A-Z) or an underscore (_).
- **Alphanumeric characters and underscores**: Subsequent characters can be letters, numbers (0-9), or underscores.
- **No spaces or special characters**: Variable names cannot contain spaces, punctuation marks, or other special characters.

Here are some examples of valid variable names:

```
name
age
file_count
user_input
```

What Goes in the Containers?

Variables in Bash can hold different types of data:
- **Strings**: Sequences of characters, such as words, sentences, or file names. String values are typically enclosed in quotes (single or double) to prevent the shell from interpreting them as commands or special characters.
- **Numbers**: Integers (whole numbers) or floating-point numbers (decimals). Bash primarily works with integers, but it can use external tools like `bc` for floating-point calculations.

Creating Variables

Variables in Bash are created automatically when you assign a value to them. There's no need to declare them explicitly beforehand, as you might do in other programming languages.

The Power of Variables

Variables are fundamental building blocks for shell scripts, allowing you to store data, perform operations on it, and reference it throughout your script. They add dynamism and flexibility to your scripts, enabling them to adapt to different inputs and conditions. In the next section, we'll explore how to assign values to these containers and unleash their full potential.

2. Assignment – Filling the Containers

With our variables created and ready to hold data, let's explore how to fill them with values. Bash offers various methods for assigning values, allowing you to store information from different sources and perform calculations to determine the content of your variables.

Direct Assignment

The most straightforward way to assign a value is using the assignment operator (=):

```
variable_name=value
```

For example:

```
name="Noah"
age=56
file_count=10
```

Important Note: There should be no spaces around the assignment operator.

Command Substitution – Capturing Output

Command substitution allows you to capture the output of a command and assign it to a variable. It uses the following syntax:

```
variable_name=$(command)
```

For example, to store the current date and time in a variable:

```
current_date=$(date)
```

This command executes the `date` command and assigns its output to the variable *current_date*.

Arithmetic Expansion – Calculating Values

Arithmetic expansion allows you to perform arithmetic operations and assign the result to a variable. It uses the following syntax:

```
variable_name=$((arithmetic_expression))
```

For example, to calculate the sum of two numbers and store the result:

```
sum=$((5 + 3))
```

This command evaluates the expression 5 + 3 and assigns the result (8) to the variable *sum*.

Filling the Data Vessels

These assignment methods provide a variety of ways to fill your variables with data, whether it's a simple string, the output of a command, or the result of a calculation. By mastering these techniques, you can create dynamic and flexible scripts that adapt to different inputs and conditions.

3. Expansions – Unleashing the Power of Variables

Variables hold the potential for dynamism and flexibility in your scripts, but to truly unleash their power, you need to understand **expansions**. Expansions are mechanisms that allow you to access and manipulate the values stored within variables, transforming them into dynamic components of your scripts.

Types of Expansions

Bash offers several types of expansions, each serving a specific purpose:
- **Parameter Expansion**: This type of expansion allows you to access the value of a variable and perform various operations on it, such as:

- Simple expansion: `$variable_name` or `${variable_name}` – Retrieves the value of the variable.
  - Substring extraction: `${variable_name:offset:length}` – Extracts a portion of the variable's value starting at the specified offset and with the specified length.
  - Pattern substitution: `${variable_name/pattern/string}` – Replaces the first occurrence of *pattern* in the variable's value with string.
  - Case modification: `${variable_name^}` – Capitalizes the first letter of the variable's value. `${variable_name^^}` – Converts the entire value to uppercase.
- **Command Substitution**: We've already encountered command substitution as a way to assign the output of a command to a variable. It can also be used within other commands or expressions to dynamically insert the result of a command. For example:

```
echo "Today's date is: $(date)"
```

- **Arithmetic Expansion**: Arithmetic expansion allows you to perform calculations within your script and use the results in expressions or assignments. For example:

```
count=$((count + 1))
if [[ $value -gt 10 ]]; then
  # Do something
fi
```

Expanding Your Horizons

Expansions are essential for creating dynamic and flexible scripts. They allow you to:

- **Access and manipulate variable values**: Extract specific information, modify strings, and perform calculations based on the content of variables.
- **Create dynamic output**: Generate text or commands based on variable values, adapting the script's behavior to different inputs and conditions.
- **Simplify expressions and commands**: Use expansions to avoid repetitive code and make your scripts more concise and readable.

By mastering the art of expansions, you unleash the true power of variables and elevate your scripting skills to new heights.

4. Constants – The Unchanging Values

While variables represent data that can change throughout the execution of a script, **constants** are like steadfast sentinels, holding values that remain fixed and unwavering. They provide a way to define values that are fundamental to your script's logic or represent unchanging parameters.

The readonly Command – Declaring Constants

To create a constant in Bash, you can use the `readonly` command:

```
readonly constant_name=value
```

For example:

```
readonly PI=3.14159
readonly MAX_USERS=10
readonly PROJECT_DIR="/home/noah/Projects"
```

Once a variable is declared as `readonly`, any attempt to modify its value will result in an error. This ensures that the constant remains truly constant throughout the script's execution.

Benefits of Constants

Using constants in your scripts offers several advantages:
- **Readability and Maintainability**: Constants make your code more readable and easier to understand by giving meaningful names to important values. Instead of using magic numbers or hardcoded strings, you can use descriptive constant names that clarify the purpose of the values.
- **Reduced Errors**: Constants help prevent accidental modification of critical values. By ensuring that these values remain constant, you reduce the risk of introducing bugs or unexpected behavior into your scripts.
- **Centralized Configuration**: Constants provide a central location for defining important values that might be used throughout your script. This makes it easier to update or modify these values in the future, as you only need to change them in one place.

Naming Conventions

A common convention is to use uppercase letters for constant names to distinguish them from regular variables:

```
readonly MAX_VALUE=100
readonly FILE_NAME="data.txt"
```

Constants – The Pillars of Stability

Constants act as pillars of stability within your scripts, ensuring that critical values remain unchanged and providing clarity and maintainability for your code. By using constants effectively, you enhance the robustness and reliability of your scripts.

5. Here Documents and Here Strings – Embedding Text Blocks

Imagine you're writing a play and need to include a long monologue for one of the characters. You wouldn't want to break up the flow of the script with multiple `echo` commands; instead, you'd prefer to embed the entire monologue as a single block of text. Here documents and here strings in Bash provide a similar capability, allowing you to embed blocks of text directly within your scripts, preserving formatting and indentation.

Here Documents – Multi-Line Marvels

A **here document** is a way to redirect a block of text as input to a command. It uses the following syntax:

```
command << delimiter
text
text
...
delimiter
```

- **command**: The command that will receive the text as input. Common choices include `cat`, `echo`, or any command that reads from standard input.
- <<: The redirection operator for here documents.

- **delimiter**: A user-defined string that marks the beginning and end of the text block. The delimiter can be any word or symbol, but it must appear on its own line and match exactly at the beginning and end of the text block.

For example, to create a file named *poem.txt* containing a short poem:

```
cat << END_POEM
Roses are red,
Violets are blue,
I'm writing a script,
Just for you.
END_POEM
```

This code block creates a here document, redirecting the four lines of the poem as input to the `cat` command, which then creates the file *poem.txt* and writes the poem into it.

Here Strings – Single-Line Snippets

Here strings provide a similar functionality but for single lines of text. They use the following syntax:

```
command <<< "text"
```

For example, to send a single line of text to the `grep` command:

```
grep "pattern" <<< "This line contains the pattern."
```

Advantages of Embedding Text

Here documents and here strings offer several benefits:
- **Preserving Formatting**: The text within the here document or here string is preserved exactly as you type it, including indentation and newlines. This makes them ideal for embedding code snippets, HTML content, or any text where formatting is important.
- **Readability**: Using here documents and here strings can improve the readability of your scripts by avoiding the need for multiple `echo` commands or complex string concatenations.

Embedding Text with Ease

Here documents and here strings provide convenient and efficient ways to embed blocks of text within your scripts, making them more readable, maintainable, and versatile.

Chapter Summary

In this chapter, we've explored the essential building blocks of shell scripting, equipping ourselves with the tools to create dynamic and powerful scripts:

- We learned about variables as named containers for storing data, understanding different data types and variable naming conventions.
- We explored various methods for assigning values to variables, including direct assignment, command substitution, and arithmetic expansion.
- We unlocked the power of expansions, discovering how to access and manipulate variable values, perform calculations, and create dynamic content.
- We introduced constants as unchanging values and learned how to define them using the `readonly` command.
- We explored techniques for embedding text blocks within scripts using here documents and here strings, preserving formatting and improving readability.

Remember, variables and constants are fundamental building blocks for creating dynamic and flexible shell scripts. By mastering these concepts and the associated techniques for assignment, expansion, and text embedding, you'll be well on your way to writing powerful and efficient scripts that automate tasks and streamline your workflow.

With these building blocks in place, you're now ready to delve into the world of flow control in the next chapter, where we'll explore how to make decisions and control the execution of your scripts using logic and loops.

Chapter 14:
Taking Control with
Logic and Loops

Imagine a skilled conductor guiding an orchestra, directing the flow of music with precise cues and gestures. Similarly, flow control in shell scripting allows you to orchestrate the execution of your scripts, making decisions based on conditions and repeating sections of code as needed.

In this chapter, we'll delve into the art of flow control, exploring the `if` statement – our conductor's baton for making decisions – and the various logical operators and comparison expressions that empower our scripts to evaluate conditions and choose different paths. Get ready to take control of your scripts and create dynamic programs that can adapt to various situations and inputs.

1. Flow Control – Directing the Script's Path

Up to this point, our scripts have executed commands in a linear fashion, one after another, from top to bottom. However, most programs require the ability to make decisions and alter their behavior based on certain conditions or inputs. This is where **flow control** comes into play, allowing you to direct the path of your script's execution and create more dynamic and responsive programs.

Types of Flow Control

There are two primary types of flow control in shell scripting:
- **Conditional Execution**: This involves making decisions and executing specific blocks of code based on whether certain conditions are met. For example, you might check if a file exists before attempting to read it, or you might display a different message depending on the user's input.
- **Looping**: This involves repeating a block of code multiple times, either a fixed number of times or until a certain condition is met. Loops are useful for tasks such as processing lists of items, iterating through files, or performing calculations until a specific result is achieved.

Flow Control Mechanisms

Bash provides several mechanisms for implementing flow control:
- `if` **statement**: The fundamental tool for conditional execution, allowing you to execute code based on the evaluation of conditions.
- **Logical operators**: Symbols like `&&` (AND), `||` (OR), and `!` (NOT) enable you to combine multiple conditions and create complex logical expressions.
- **Comparison expressions**: These expressions allow you to compare values and determine their relationship (e.g., equal, not equal, greater than, less than).
- **Looping constructs**: Bash provides several looping constructs, including `while`, `until`, and `for`, which we'll explore in detail in the next chapter.

The Power of Control

Flow control empowers your scripts to make decisions, adapt to different situations, and perform complex tasks. By mastering the art of flow control, you'll transform your scripts from simple sequences of commands into dynamic and responsive programs capable of handling a wide range of scenarios.

2. if Statements – Making Decisions

The `if` statement is the cornerstone of conditional execution in shell scripting. It allows your script to evaluate a condition and execute a block of code only if the condition is true. It's like a fork in the road, guiding your script's execution based on the outcome of a decision.

The Basic Structure

The basic syntax of an `if` statement is as follows:

```
if condition; then
  # Code to execute if the condition is true
fi
```

Let's break down the components:
- **if**: The keyword that introduces the `if` statement.
- **condition**: An expression that evaluates to either true or false. This could be a comparison expression, a test of a file's existence, or any other expression that returns a boolean value.
- **then**: The keyword that separates the condition from the code block to be executed.
- **# Code to execute if the condition is true**: The block of code that will be executed only if the condition evaluates to true.
- **fi**: The keyword that marks the end of the `if` statement.

Example: Checking File Existence

```
filename="data.txt"

if [ -f "$filename" ]; then
  echo "File '$filename' exists."
fi
```

In this example, the script checks if the file *data.txt* exists using the `-f` test within the [ ] (test) command. If the file exists, the condition evaluates to true, and the `echo` command is executed, displaying a message indicating the file's existence. If the file doesn't exist, the condition is false, and the code within the if block is skipped.

Making Informed Choices

The if statement empowers your scripts to make decisions based on conditions, allowing for more dynamic and adaptable behavior. In the upcoming sections, we'll explore how to combine conditions using logical operators and delve into different types of comparison expressions to evaluate various conditions.

3. The else Clause – Providing an Alternative Path

The if statement allows your script to take action when a condition is true, but what about when the condition is false? The else clause provides an alternative path for your script's execution, specifying a block of code to be executed if the if condition evaluates to false. It's like having a backup plan, ensuring that your script always has a course of action, regardless of the outcome of the decision.

The Structure with else

Here's the syntax of an if statement with an else clause:

```
if condition; then
  # Code to execute if the condition is true
else
  # Code to execute if the condition is false
fi
```

Example: Handling File Absence

```
filename="data.txt"

if [ -f "$filename" ]; then
  echo "File '$filename' exists."
else
  echo "File '$filename' does not exist."
fi
```

In this enhanced example, if the file *data.txt* doesn't exist, the `else` clause steps in and executes the `echo` command, informing the user about the file's absence.

Providing a Safety Net

The `else` clause acts as a safety net, ensuring your script can handle situations where the initial condition is not met. It allows you to provide alternative actions or informative messages, making your scripts more robust and user-friendly.

4. The elif Clause – Exploring Multiple Options

The `if` statement with an `else` clause handles a binary decision – either the condition is true, or it's false. But what if you need to consider multiple possibilities? The `elif` clause, short for "else if," allows you to chain multiple conditions, creating a series of decision points for your script's execution. It's like having multiple forks in the road, each leading to a different destination based on the evaluation of different conditions.

The Structure with elif

Here's the syntax of an `if` statement with `elif` and `else` clauses:

```
if condition1; then
    # Code to execute if condition1 is true
elif condition2; then
    # Code to execute if condition2 is true
elif condition3; then
    # Code to execute if condition3 is true
else
    # Code to execute if none of the conditions are true
fi
```

Example: Evaluating User Input

```
read -p "Enter a number: " number

if [[ "$number" -eq 1 ]]; then
```

```
  echo "You entered one."
elif [[ "$number" -eq 2 ]]; then
  echo "You entered two."
elif [[ "$number" -eq 3 ]]; then
  echo "You entered three."
else
  echo "You entered a different number."
fi
```

In this example, the script prompts the user to enter a number. The `if` statement then evaluates the input using multiple `elif` clauses to check if the number is 1, 2, or 3. If none of the conditions match, the `else` clause provides a default message.

Expanding Decision-Making

The `elif` clause extends the decision-making capabilities of the `if` statement, allowing you to handle multiple scenarios and create more complex and adaptable scripts.

5. Logical Operators – Combining Conditions

While individual conditions within an `if` statement provide basic decision-making capabilities, **logical operators** allow you to combine multiple conditions and create more complex and nuanced expressions. They are like the conjunctions in a sentence, connecting individual clauses to form a complete thought.

The Trio of Logical Operators

Bash provides three primary logical operators:
*   **&& (AND)**: This operator combines two conditions, and the combined expression is true only if **both** conditions are true. It's like saying, "I want to eat a cookie AND drink milk." Both desires need to be fulfilled for the overall statement to be true.
*   **|| (OR)**: This operator combines two conditions, and the combined expression is true if **at least one** of the conditions is true. It's like saying, "I want tea OR coffee." As long as you get one of the beverages, the statement is true.
*   **! (NOT)**: This operator negates a condition, reversing its truth value. For example, `! -f file.txt` would be true if the file *file.txt* does not exist.

161

Building Complex Expressions

Logical operators allow you to create complex expressions that evaluate multiple conditions. For example:

```
if [[ -f "$filename" && -r "$filename" ]]; then
  echo "File '$filename' exists and is readable."
fi
```

This `if` statement uses the `&&` operator to combine two conditions: the file must exist (-f), and it must be readable (-r). Only if both conditions are true will the message be displayed.

Examples of Logical Combinations

Here are a few more examples of using logical operators:
- Check if a file exists and is not empty: `[[ -s "$filename" && -f "$filename" ]]`
- Check if a user is either "root" or "noah": `[[ "$USER" == "root" || "$USER" == "noah" ]]`
- Check if a variable is not empty: `[[ -n "$variable" ]]`

Mastering Logical Thinking

Logical operators are essential for building complex decision-making structures in your scripts. By understanding how to combine conditions with AND, OR, and NOT, you can create scripts that respond to a wide range of scenarios and make intelligent choices based on multiple factors.

6. Comparison Expressions – Evaluating Conditions

Logical operators allow us to combine conditions, but how do we actually evaluate those conditions? **Comparison expressions** are the tools we use to compare values and determine their relationship, forming the building blocks of our logical tests.

Types of Comparisons

Bash provides various types of comparison expressions for different data types and scenarios:
- String Comparisons:

- ○ **= or ==**: Checks if two strings are equal. For example, [["$str1" == "$str2"]] is true if the values of *str1* and *str2* are identical.
  - ○ **!=**: Checks if two strings are not equal.
  - ○ **< and >**: Compare strings lexicographically (alphabetical order).
  - ○ **-z**: Checks if a string is empty (zero length).
  - ○ **-n**: Checks if a string is not empty.
- • Numeric Comparisons:
  - ○ **-eq**: Equal to.
  - ○ **-ne**: Not equal to.
  - ○ **-lt**: Less than.
  - ○ **-gt**: Greater than.
  - ○ **-le**: Less than or equal to.
  - ○ **-ge**: Greater than or equal to.
- • File Tests:
  - ○ **-e**: Checks if a file exists.
  - ○ **-f**: Checks if a file is a regular file (not a directory or special file).
  - ○ **-d**: Checks if a file is a directory.
  - ○ **-r**: Checks if a file is readable by the current user.
  - ○ **-w**: Checks if a file is writable by the current user.
  - ○ **-x**: Checks if a file is executable by the current user.

Examples of Comparisons

Here are a few examples of using comparison expressions:

```
# String comparisons
if [[ "$user_input" == "yes" ]]; then
  # Do something
fi

# Numeric comparisons
if (( count > 10 )); then
  echo "Count is greater than 10."
fi

# File tests
if [ -d "$directory_name" ]; then
  echo "Directory '$directory_name' exists."
fi
```

Evaluating the Relationships

Comparison expressions are the building blocks of logical tests, allowing your scripts to evaluate conditions and make decisions based on the relationships between values. By understanding the different types of comparisons and their syntax, you can create scripts that respond intelligently to various inputs and situations.

7. test and [[ ]] – Evaluating Expressions

We have our comparison expressions ready to evaluate conditions, but we need a mechanism to actually perform the evaluation and determine their truth value. The test command and its more modern equivalent, [[ ]], are the tools we use for this purpose, acting as judges in our scripts' decision-making processes.

The test Command

The test command evaluates an expression and returns an exit status indicating whether the expression is true (exit status 0) or false (exit status 1). It has the following syntax:

```
test expression
```

For example, to check if a file exists:

```
if test -f "myfile.txt"; then
   echo "File 'myfile.txt' exists."
fi
```

The [[ ]] Compound Command

The [[ ]] compound command provides a more modern and versatile syntax for evaluating expressions. It's generally preferred over test due to its improved readability and additional features. The syntax is similar to test:

```
if [[ expression ]]; then
   # Code to execute if the expression is true
fi
```

For example:

164

```
if [[ "$user_input" == "yes" ]]; then
  echo "You entered 'yes'."
fi
```

Advantages of [[ ]]

- **Improved Readability**: The [[ ]] syntax is more readable and resembles natural language expressions.
- **Enhanced Functionality**: [[ ]] supports additional features like regular expression matching and pattern matching with wildcards.
- **Word Splitting**: Inside [[ ]], word splitting is not performed, eliminating the need for quoting variables in many cases.

Choosing Your Evaluation Tool

Both test and [[ ]] serve the same fundamental purpose of evaluating expressions. However, [[ ]] is generally preferred due to its improved readability and enhanced functionality.

8. (( )) – Arithmetic Evaluation

While test and [[ ]] excel at evaluating string and file-related expressions, the (( )) compound command provides a specialized environment for performing arithmetic evaluations and comparisons. It's like having a built-in calculator within your scripts, allowing you to perform calculations and make decisions based on numerical values.

Arithmetic Expressions within (( ))

The (( )) command allows you to evaluate arithmetic expressions using a C-like syntax:

```
if (( expression )); then
  # Code to execute if the expression is true (non-zero result)
fi
```

For example, to check if a variable count is greater than 10:

```
if (( count > 10 )); then
  echo "Count is greater than 10."
fi
```

Arithmetic Operators

(( )) supports a wide range of arithmetic operators:
- **Basic arithmetic:** +, -, *, /, % (modulo)
- **Increment and decrement:** ++, --
- **Bitwise operators:** &, |, ^, ~, <<, >>
- **Assignment operators:** =, +=, -=, *=, /=, %=

Comparisons within (( ))

You can also use comparison operators within (( )) for numerical comparisons:
- ==: Equal to.
- !=: Not equal to.
- <: Less than.
- >: Greater than.
- <=: Less than or equal to.
- >=: Greater than or equal to.

Example: Calculating Factorial

```
read -p "Enter a number: " num
factorial=1


for (( i=1; i<=num; i++ )); do
  factorial=$((factorial * i))
done


echo "The factorial of $num is $factorial"
```

This script demonstrates using (( )) for arithmetic calculations and a **for** loop (which we'll explore in the next chapter) to calculate the factorial of a number.

A Numerical Powerhouse

The `(( ))` command, with its C-like syntax and support for various arithmetic operations and comparisons, is a valuable tool for performing calculations and making decisions based on numerical values in your shell scripts.

Chapter Summary

In this chapter, we've taken control of our scripts' destinies by mastering the art of flow control, enabling them to make decisions and adapt to different situations:

- We explored the concept of flow control and its importance in creating dynamic and responsive scripts.
- We learned about conditional execution using the `if` statement and its various forms, including `elif` and `else`, allowing our scripts to make choices based on the evaluation of conditions.
- We discovered the power of logical operators (`&&`, `||`, `!`) for combining conditions and creating complex logical expressions.
- We delved into comparison expressions, understanding how to compare strings, numbers, and file attributes using various operators and tests.
- We explored the tools for evaluating expressions, including the `test` command, the `[[ ]]` compound command, and the `(( ))` command for arithmetic evaluation.

Flow control is a fundamental concept in shell scripting, empowering you to create scripts that can adapt to different scenarios, make intelligent decisions, and perform complex tasks based on various conditions and inputs.

In the next chapter, we'll explore another essential aspect of flow control – looping – and learn how to repeat sections of code to process data, iterate through files, and perform repetitive tasks with efficiency and precision.

Chapter 15:
Looping Like a Pro

Imagine a tireless worker who can perform repetitive tasks with unwavering precision, never complaining or taking a break. In the realm of shell scripting, **loops** are those tireless workers, allowing you to repeat sections of code multiple times, automating tedious tasks and processing data with efficiency and accuracy.

In this chapter, we'll explore the art of looping, mastering the `while`, `until`, and `for` constructs like seasoned choreographers. You'll learn to create loops that iterate over numbers, process lists of items, and read lines from files, all while maintaining control over the flow of execution. So, prepare to unlock the power of repetition and become a looping maestro!

1. Looping – The Art of Repetition

Repetition is a fundamental concept in both the physical and digital worlds. From the rhythmic beat of a heart to the automated assembly lines in factories, countless processes rely on repeating a series of actions to achieve a desired outcome. In shell scripting, **looping** provides a way to automate these repetitions, allowing your scripts to perform tasks multiple times, process data efficiently, and adapt to varying inputs and conditions.

The Benefits of Looping

Looping offers several advantages:
- **Automation**: Loops eliminate the need to manually repeat commands or code blocks, saving time and effort.
- **Efficiency**: Loops allow you to process large amounts of data or perform complex calculations with minimal code, improving the efficiency of your scripts.
- **Flexibility**: Loops can be used to iterate over a fixed number of items or continue until a certain condition is met, providing flexibility in handling different scenarios.
- **Data Processing**: Loops are essential for tasks like reading lines from files, processing lists of items, or performing calculations that require multiple iterations.

Types of Loops in Bash

Bash provides three main looping constructs, each with its own unique characteristics and use cases:
- `while` **loop**: This loop continues to execute as long as a specified condition is true. It's like a persistent traveler who keeps walking as long as the path ahead is clear.
- `until` **loop**: This loop continues to execute until a specified condition becomes true. It's like a determined seeker who keeps searching until they find what they're looking for.
- `for` **loop**: This versatile loop iterates over a sequence of items, such as a list of words, a range of numbers, or the contents of a file. It's like a methodical organizer, processing each item in turn.

The Power of Repetition

Looping is a cornerstone of scripting, enabling you to automate repetitive tasks, process data efficiently, and create dynamic and adaptable scripts. In the following sections, we'll explore each looping construct in detail and discover how to wield their power to automate the mundane and transform your scripts into efficient workhorses.

2. while Loop – Repeating Until a Condition is False

The while loop is like a persistent hiker who continues their journey as long as the trail ahead remains clear. In shell scripting, a while loop repeatedly executes a block of code as long as a specified condition evaluates to true.

The Structure of a while Loop

The basic syntax of a while loop is:

```
while condition; do
  # Code to execute repeatedly
done
```

Here's how it works:
1.   The condition is evaluated.
2.   If the condition is true, the code block within the do...done section is executed.
3.   After the code block is executed, the condition is evaluated again.
4.   Steps 2 and 3 are repeated until the condition becomes false.
5.   Once the condition is false, the loop terminates, and the script continues with the next statement after the done keyword.

Example: Counting to Ten

```
Count=1

while [[ $count -le 10 ]]; do
  echo "$count"
  count=$((count + 1))
done
```

```
echo "Finished counting."
```

This script initializes a variable `count` to 1 and then uses a `while` loop to repeatedly print the value of `count` and increment it by 1 until `count` reaches 11.

while Loop Use Cases

`while` loops are useful for:
- **Iterating over a range of numbers**: As demonstrated in the previous example, `while` loops are perfect for counting up or down or performing calculations that require multiple iterations.
- **Processing user input**: You can use a `while` loop to repeatedly prompt the user for input until they provide a valid response or choose to exit.
- **Reading data from a file**: A `while` loop can be used to read lines from a file until the end of the file is reached.

The Persistence of while

The `while` loop is a powerful tool for automating repetitive tasks and creating dynamic scripts that adapt to changing conditions. By understanding its structure and capabilities, you can harness its persistence to tackle a wide range of scripting challenges.

3. until Loop – Repeating Until a Condition is True

The `until` loop is like a determined detective who tirelessly investigates clues until they crack the case. In shell scripting, an `until` loop repeatedly executes a block of code until a specified condition becomes true. It's the opposite of a `while` loop, which continues as long as a condition is true.

The Structure of an until Loop

The basic syntax of an `until` loop is:

```
until condition; do
  # Code to execute repeatedly
done
```

Here's how it works:
1. The `condition` is evaluated.
2. If the `condition` is false, the code block within the `do...done` section is executed.
3. After the code block is executed, the `condition` is evaluated again.
4. Steps 2 and 3 are repeated until the `condition` becomes true.
5. Once the `condition` is true, the loop terminates, and the script continues with the next statement after the `done` keyword.

Example: Waiting for a File

```
filename="data.txt"

until [ -f "$filename" ]; do
  echo "Waiting for file '$filename' to exist…"
  sleep 5
done
echo "File '$filename' found!"
```

This script uses an `until` loop to repeatedly check if the file *data.txt* exists. As long as the file is not found, the loop will display a message and wait for 5 seconds before checking again. Once the file appears, the loop terminates, and a success message is displayed.

until vs. while – Choosing the Right Loop

The choice between `while` and `until` often depends on the clarity and logic of the condition you want to express. If you want to continue looping as long as a condition is true, use `while`. If you want to continue looping until a condition becomes true, use `until`. Both loops can achieve the same results, but choosing the appropriate one can make your code more readable and easier to understand.

The Determination of until

The `until` loop, with its unwavering determination to continue until a condition is met, is a valuable tool for scripting tasks that involve waiting for events, checking for file availability, or repeating actions until a specific state is reached.

4. for Loop – Iterating Over a Sequence

The for loop is like a methodical organizer, meticulously processing each item in a collection. It's a versatile tool for iterating over a sequence of items, such as a list of words, a range of numbers, or the files in a directory.

Forms of the for Loop

Bash offers two main forms of the for loop:
- **Traditional for loop**: This form iterates over a list of words.

```
for variable in list_of_words; do
  # Code to execute for each word
done
```

- **C-style for loop**: This form iterates over a range of numbers using a C-like syntax.

```
for (( initialization; condition; increment )); do
  # Code to execute for each number in the range
done
```

Traditional for Loop Examples

Here are a few examples of using the traditional for loop:
- Iterating over a list of filenames:

```
for file in *.txt; do
  echo "Processing file: $file"
  # Do something with the file
done
```

- Iterating over a list of words:

```
for word in hello world scripting; do
  echo "$word"
done
```

C-style for Loop Examples

Here are a few examples of using the C-style `for` loop:

- Counting from 1 to 10:

```
for (( i=1; i<=10; i++ )); do
  echo "$i"
done
```

- Iterating over even numbers:

```
for (( i=0; i<=10; i+=2 )); do
  echo "$i"
done
```

The Power of Iteration

The `for` loop, with its different forms and ability to iterate over various sequences, is a versatile tool for automating tasks that involve processing lists of items, iterating through files, or performing calculations with a specific number of repetitions.

5. Controlling the Flow – break and continue

While loops provide a powerful mechanism for repetition, sometimes you need to exert finer control over their execution. The `break` and `continue` commands act as traffic signals within your loops, allowing you to either stop the loop entirely or skip to the next iteration.

break – Exiting the Loop

The `break` command immediately terminates the current loop, regardless of whether the loop condition is still true. It's like hitting the emergency stop button, bringing the loop to a halt and resuming execution with the statement following the loop.

Here's an example of using `break` to exit a loop when a specific condition is met:

```
while read line; do
  if [[ "$line" == "END" ]]; then
  break
```

```
  fi
  echo "$line"
done < data.txt
```

This script reads lines from the file *data.txt* and prints them to the screen. If it encounters a line containing only the word "END", the break command terminates the loop, and the script exits.

continue – Skipping to the Next Iteration

The `continue` command skips the remaining statements in the current loop iteration and jumps to the beginning of the next iteration. It's like taking a detour, bypassing a section of the loop but continuing the overall journey.

Here's an example of using `continue` to skip lines starting with a "#" (comment lines):

```
while read line; do
  if [[ "$line" =~ ^# ]]; then
    continue
  fi
  echo "$line"
done < config.txt
```

This script reads lines from a configuration file (*config.txt*) and prints them to the screen. If a line starts with a #, the `continue` command skips it, and the loop moves on to the next line.

Fine-Tuning Loop Execution

The `break` and `continue` commands provide finer control over the flow of execution within loops, allowing you to exit loops prematurely, skip specific iterations, or handle exceptional cases. By using these commands effectively, you can create more robust and adaptable scripts that respond intelligently to various conditions and inputs.

6. Looping Applications – Automating the Mundane

Loops are not just theoretical constructs; they are the workhorses of automation, allowing you to perform repetitive tasks with efficiency and precision. Let's explore some practical applications of loops in shell scripts, transforming mundane and tedious tasks into automated workflows.

Processing Files in a Directory

Imagine you need to convert all `.jpg` images in a directory to `.png` format. You could use a `for` loop to iterate over the files and perform the conversion:

```
for image in *.jpg; do
  convert "$image" "${image%.jpg}.png"
done
```

This script loops through all files with the `.jpg` extension, using the `convert` command (from the ImageMagick package) to convert each image to a `.png` file with the same name.

Reading Lines from a File

Loops are often used to process text files line by line. For example, to extract the usernames from the */etc/passwd* file:

```
while IFS=':' read -r username password uid gid fullname homedir shell; do
  echo "$username"
done < /etc/passwd
```

This script uses a `while` loop with the `read` command to read each line of */etc/passwd*, splitting the line into fields based on the colon (:) delimiter and assigning the first field (username) to the variable *username*. The script then prints each username to the screen.

Performing Repetitive Calculations

Loops can be used to perform calculations that require multiple iterations. For example, to calculate the sum of the first 100 natural numbers:

```
sum=0

for ((i=1; i<=100; i++)); do
  sum=$((sum + i))
```

176

```
done

echo "The sum is: $sum"
```

This script uses a C-style `for` loop to iterate from 1 to 100, adding each number to the *sum* variable.

Interacting with the User

Loops can create interactive scripts that prompt the user for input and process it within the loop. For example, a simple guessing game:

```
secret_number=$((RANDOM % 100 + 1))

while true; do
  read -p "Guess the number (1-100): " guess
  if (( guess == secret_number )); then
    echo "Congratulations! You guessed it!"
    break
  elif (( guess < secret_number )); then
    echo "Too low. Try again."
  else
    echo "Too high. Try again."
  fi
done
```

This script uses a `while` loop to repeatedly ask the user for a guess until they guess the correct number.

Automating with Loops

These examples showcase the versatility of loops for automating tasks, processing data, and creating interactive scripts. As you explore and experiment, you'll discover countless ways to leverage the power of loops to transform mundane and repetitive tasks into efficient and automated workflows.

Chapter Summary

In this chapter, we've embraced the art of repetition and become looping virtuosos, wielding the power of `while`, `until`, and `for` to automate tasks and process data with efficiency:

- We explored the concept of looping and its advantages for automation, efficiency, and flexibility in shell scripting.
- We learned how to use `while` loops to repeat code as long as a condition is true, creating loops that count, process user input, or read data from files.
- We discovered the `until` loop, which continues until a condition becomes true, providing an alternative approach to repetition.
- We mastered the versatile `for` loop, iterating over lists of words, ranges of numbers, and file contents with both traditional and C-style syntax.
- We learned to control the flow of execution within loops using `break` to exit loops prematurely and `continue` to skip to the next iteration.
- We explored practical applications of loops for automating tasks, processing files, performing calculations, and creating interactive scripts.

Loops are indispensable tools for any shell scripter, enabling you to automate repetitive tasks, process data efficiently, and create dynamic and adaptable programs. By mastering the art of looping, you'll unlock new levels of productivity and transform your scripts into powerful automation engines.

With looping constructs under your command, you're now ready to explore the world of arrays in the next chapter, where you'll discover how to manage collections of data and further enhance the capabilities of your scripts.

Chapter 16:

Scripting with Arrays

Imagine organizing a collection of spices in your kitchen – you wouldn't simply toss them all into a drawer; instead, you'd use a spice rack with individual compartments for each spice, allowing you to easily locate and access the one you need. **Arrays** in shell scripting offer a similar organizational structure, providing a way to store and manage collections of data efficiently.

In this chapter, we'll explore the world of arrays, discovering how to create these data containers, access their individual elements, and perform various operations on them, such as sorting, adding, and deleting. We'll delve into different types of arrays, including indexed arrays and associative arrays, and uncover their power for organizing and processing data within your scripts. So, prepare to become a master organizer and unleash the power of arrays in your scripting endeavors!

1. Arrays – Organizing Your Data

In the previous chapters, we've encountered variables as containers for storing single values. However, when dealing with multiple pieces of related data, such as a list of names, a collection of file sizes, or a set of configuration options, individual variables can become cumbersome and inefficient. This is where **arrays** come to the rescue, providing a structured way to organize and manage collections of data.

Arrays vs. Scalar Variables

Unlike scalar variables, which hold a single value, arrays can store multiple values within a single variable. Think of an array as a collection of compartments, each holding a separate piece of data. These compartments, called **elements**, are accessed using an **index** or **key**, allowing you to retrieve or modify specific values within the array.

The Benefits of Arrays

Arrays offer several advantages for data management:
- **Organization**: Arrays provide a structured way to group related data, making your code more organized and easier to understand.
- **Efficiency**: Instead of creating multiple variables for each piece of data, you can store them all within a single array, improving efficiency and reducing code clutter.
- **Iteration**: Arrays work seamlessly with loops, allowing you to easily iterate over the elements and perform operations on each one.
- **Flexibility**: Arrays can be used to store various types of data, including strings, numbers, and even other arrays, providing flexibility in data representation.

Types of Arrays

Bash supports two main types of arrays:
- **Indexed arrays**: Elements are accessed using numerical indices, starting from zero. They are like numbered storage bins, where each bin holds a specific item.
- **Associative arrays**: Elements are accessed using string keys, allowing you to create key-value pairs. They are like dictionaries, where each word (key) is associated with a definition (value).

Mastering Data Organization

Arrays are powerful tools for organizing and managing data within your scripts. By understanding the different types of arrays and their capabilities, you'll be able to create more efficient, structured, and adaptable scripts that handle complex data with ease.

2. Indexed Arrays – Ordered Collections

Indexed arrays are the most basic type of array in Bash. They are ordered collections of elements, with each element accessible using a numerical index. Think of an indexed array as a row of numbered boxes, each containing a separate piece of data. You can access any element directly by specifying its index, starting from zero for the first element.

Creating and Initializing Indexed Arrays

There are several ways to create and initialize indexed arrays in Bash:
- Direct assignment:

```
array_name=(value1 value2 value3 ...)
```

This syntax creates an array named *array_name* and assigns the specified values to its elements, starting with index 0 for the first element. For example:

```
fruits=("apple" "banana" "cherry")
```

- Individual element assignment:

```
array_name[index]=value
```

This syntax assigns a specific value to an element at a given index. For example, to assign the value "grape" to the fourth element (index 3):

```
fruits[3]="grape"
```

- Using a loop:

```
for i in {0..4}; do
 numbers[i]=$i
done
```

- Using brace expansion:

```
numbers=({0..4})
```

This example utilizes brace expansion to generate a sequence of numbers from 0 to 4 and assigns them to the *numbers* array.

Accessing Array Elements

To access an individual element of an indexed array, you use the array name followed by the index in square brackets:

```
${array_name[index]}
```

For example, to print the second element (index 1) of the *fruits* array:

```
echo ${fruits[1]} # Output: banana
```

Important Note: The curly braces around the array name are necessary to prevent ambiguity and ensure the shell interprets the expression correctly.

Indexed Arrays – Orderly Data Storage

Indexed arrays provide a simple and efficient way to store and access ordered collections of data. By understanding how to create, initialize, and access elements in indexed arrays, you gain a valuable tool for managing and processing data within your scripts.

3. Array Operations – Manipulating the Collection

Arrays are not static entities; they are dynamic collections that you can manipulate and modify as needed. Bash provides several operations for working with arrays, allowing you to determine their size, sort their elements, add new elements, and remove unwanted ones.

Determining Array Length

To find the number of elements in an array, you can use the # symbol with the array name and the @ symbol in parameter expansion:

```
${#array_name[@]}
```

For example, to find the number of elements in the *fruits* array:

```
echo ${#fruits[@]}  # Output: 4
```

Sorting Arrays

Bash doesn't have a built-in command for sorting arrays, but you can achieve sorting using a combination of loops and the **sort** command:

```
sorted_array=($(for element in "${array_name[@]}"; do
  echo "$element"
done | sort))
```

This code snippet creates a new array named *sorted_array* and populates it with the sorted elements of the original array (*array_name*).

Adding Elements

To add new elements to the end of an array, you can use the += operator:

```
array_name+=(new_element1 new_element2 ...)
```

For example, to add "mango" and "pineapple" to the *fruits* array:

```
fruits+=("mango" "pineapple")
```

Deleting Elements

To remove elements from an array, you can use the **unset** command:
• Remove a specific element:

```
unset array_name[index]
```

For example, to remove the third element (index 2) from the *fruits* array:

```
unset fruits[2]
```

- Remove the entire array:

```
unset array_name
```

Mastering Array Manipulation

These operations allow you to manipulate and modify arrays as needed, providing flexibility and control over your data collections. By understanding how to perform these operations, you can adapt your arrays to changing requirements and ensure efficient data management within your scripts.

4. Associative Arrays – Key-Value Pairs

While indexed arrays excel at storing ordered collections of data, **associative arrays** offer a more flexible approach, allowing you to associate values with string keys, creating key-value pairs. They are like dictionaries, where each word (key) has a corresponding definition (value).

Creating and Initializing Associative Arrays

Associative arrays require explicit declaration using the `declare` command with the `-A` option:

```
declare -A array_name
```

You can then assign values using key-value pairs:

```
array_name[key]=value
```

For example, to create an associative array for storing color codes:

```
declare -A colors
colors[red]="#ff0000"
colors[green]="#00ff00"
colors[blue]="#0000ff"
```

Accessing Elements by Key

To access an element in an associative array, use the array name and the key within square brackets:

```
${array_name[key]}
```

For example, to print the color code for blue:

```
echo ${colors[blue]}  # Output: #0000ff
```

Advantages of Associative Arrays

Associative arrays offer several advantages over indexed arrays:
- **Meaningful Keys**: Using descriptive keys makes your code more readable and easier to understand, as the keys convey the meaning of the associated values.
- **Flexibility**: You can use any string as a key, allowing you to create custom mappings and associations that suit your specific needs.
- **Dynamic Structure**: You can add or remove key-value pairs dynamically without worrying about maintaining a specific order or index sequence.

Key-Value Power

Associative arrays provide a powerful and flexible way to manage data that can be associated with descriptive keys. They are ideal for creating dictionaries, lookup tables, and other structures where the relationship between keys and values is important.

5. Arrays in Action – Practical Applications

Arrays, with their ability to organize and manage collections of data, are versatile tools that can be applied to a wide range of scripting scenarios. Let's explore some practical examples of how arrays can enhance your scripts and streamline data processing tasks.

Storing and Processing Lists

Arrays are perfect for storing and processing lists of items, such as usernames, filenames, or configuration options:

```
# Store a list of usernames
usernames=("noah" "alice" "bob")

# Loop through the usernames and display a greeting
for user in "${usernames[@]}"; do
  echo "Hello, $user!"
done
```

Creating Lookup Tables and Dictionaries

Associative arrays are ideal for creating lookup tables or dictionaries:

```
# Create a dictionary of country codes
declare -A country_codes
country_codes[US]="United States"
country_codes[CA]="Canada"
country_codes[UK]="United Kingdom"

# Look up a country code
read -p "Enter a country code: " code
echo "${country_codes[$code]}"
```

Building Menus and Handling User Input

Arrays can simplify the creation of menus and the handling of user input:

```
options=("Display system information" "Check disk usage" "Exit")

select choice in "${options[@]}"; do
  case $REPLY in
    1) # Display system information
      # ...
```

```
        ;;
    2) # Check disk usage
        # ...
        ;;
    3) echo "Exiting…"
        break
        ;;
    *) echo "Invalid choice."
    esac
done
```

This script uses an indexed array to store menu options and the `select` construct to present them to the user.

Processing and Analyzing Data Sets

Arrays are invaluable for processing and analyzing data sets, such as CSV files or log files:

```
# Read data from a CSV file into an array
while IFS=',' read -r name age city; do
  data+=([name]="$name" [age]="$age" [city]="$city")
done < data.csv

# Process the data
for key in "${!data[@]}"; do
  echo "$key: ${data[$key]}"
done
```

This script reads data from a CSV file and stores it in an associative array, using the first field (name) as the key. It then loops through the array and displays each key-value pair.

Arrays – Organizing for Efficiency

Arrays provide a powerful and versatile mechanism for organizing and managing data within your scripts. By understanding the different types of arrays and their operations, you can create more efficient, structured, and adaptable scripts that handle complex data with ease.

Chapter Summary

In this chapter, we've ventured into the realm of data structures and discovered the power of arrays for organizing and managing collections of data within our scripts:

- We explored the concept of arrays as containers for storing multiple values, contrasting them with scalar variables and highlighting their advantages for data organization and efficiency.
- We learned about **indexed arrays**, ordered collections of elements accessible using numerical indices, and explored methods for creating, initializing, and accessing their elements.
- We mastered essential **array operations**, such as determining array length, sorting elements, adding new elements, and deleting unwanted ones.
- We delved into the world of **associative arrays**, which use string keys to access values, creating flexible and dynamic key-value pairs similar to dictionaries.
- We explored practical applications of arrays in scripts, from storing and processing lists of data to creating lookup tables, building menus, and analyzing data sets.

Arrays are fundamental tools for any shell scripter, providing a structured and efficient way to manage data collections. By understanding the different types of arrays, their operations, and their applications, you can create more organized, adaptable, and powerful scripts that handle complex data with ease.

With the power of arrays at your disposal, you're now ready to move on to the next chapter, where we'll shift our focus to handling permissions programmatically within our scripts, ensuring data security and access control.

Chapter 17:
Permission in Scripts

Imagine building a house with unlocked doors and windows – anyone could enter and do as they please, potentially causing damage or compromising the security of your belongings. Similarly, shell scripts without proper permission controls can pose security risks, allowing unauthorized access to files, execution of unintended actions, and potential harm to your system.

In this chapter, we'll explore the crucial task of **handling permissions programmatically** within our scripts. We'll learn to check for proper access rights before performing actions, modify permissions as needed, and cautiously utilize tools like sudo for elevated privileges. By mastering these techniques, you'll ensure that your scripts operate securely and responsibly, safeguarding your data and system from unauthorized access and potential harm.

1. Permissions and Scripts – A Security Imperative

As we've learned in chapter 6, file permissions and ownership are the gatekeepers of the Linux file system, controlling access and ensuring data security. When it comes to shell scripts, these access control mechanisms become even more critical, as scripts often perform actions that can have significant consequences for your system.

Inherited Permissions – The Script's Identity

When a script is executed, it inherits the permissions and ownership of the user who runs it. This means that the script can access files and directories with the same level of privilege as the executing user.

For example, if you, as a regular user, run a script that attempts to modify a system configuration file, the script will fail because it doesn't have the necessary permissions to write to that file. However, if the same script is executed by the superuser (root), it will succeed, as the superuser has elevated privileges to access and modify system files.

Security Concerns – The Risks of Excessive Permissions

Granting scripts overly broad permissions can pose security risks:
- **Unauthorized Access**: If a script with write permissions is compromised, an attacker could modify the script to perform malicious actions, such as deleting files, stealing data, or installing malware.
- **Accidental Damage**: Even without malicious intent, a script with excessive permissions could inadvertently modify or delete important files, leading to data loss or system instability.
- **Privilege Escalation**: If a script with *setuid* or *setgid* permissions is poorly written or contains vulnerabilities, it could be exploited by an attacker to gain elevated privileges and compromise the system.

The Principle of Least Privilege

To mitigate these risks, it's crucial to adhere to the **principle of least privilege** when working with scripts. This principle dictates that scripts should be granted only the minimum permissions necessary to perform their intended tasks. By limiting permissions, you minimize the potential for damage in case of errors, security breaches, or unintended consequences.

In the following sections, we'll explore techniques for handling permissions within your scripts, ensuring that they operate securely and responsibly.

2. Potential Issues – Navigating Permission Pitfalls

As your scripts become more complex and interact with various files and directories, you might encounter situations where permissions become obstacles or potential security hazards. Let's explore some common scenarios where script permissions can cause issues and discuss ways to navigate these pitfalls.

Accessing Restricted Files

Imagine you've written a script that needs to read data from a file owned by another user. If your script runs with your regular user permissions, it won't have access to the file, resulting in an error.

```
[noah@linux_lab ~]$ cat /home/otheruser/data.txt
cat: /home/otheruser/data.txt: Permission denied
```

In this case, you have a few options:
- **Request access**: Ask the file owner to grant you read permissions to the file.
- **Change ownership**: If you have superuser privileges, you can change the ownership of the file to yourself or a group you belong to.
- **Use sudo**: You can temporarily elevate your privileges using sudo to read the file, but this should be done with caution and only if necessary.

Modifying System Files

Scripts that need to modify system files or perform administrative tasks typically require superuser privileges. Running such scripts as a regular user will result in permission denied errors.

For example, a script that updates a system configuration file:

```
[noah@linux_lab ~]$ echo "new_setting=value" >> /etc/config.conf
bash: /etc/config.conf: Permission denied
```

In this scenario, you can either:
- **Run the script with sudo**: This allows the script to execute with elevated privileges and modify the system file.
- **Modify the script to use tools like visudo** to grant specific users permission to execute the script with sudo for the required commands.

Handling Sensitive Data

Scripts that handle sensitive data, such as passwords, financial information, or personal records, require careful consideration of permissions. It's crucial to restrict access to these scripts and the data they handle to prevent unauthorized disclosure or modification.

Here are some strategies:

- **Limit script permissions**: Grant execute permissions only to authorized users, and avoid using *setuid* or *setgid* permissions.
- **Store sensitive data securely**: Use encrypted files or databases to store confidential information.
- **Validate user input**: Ensure that the script validates any user-provided data to prevent injection attacks or unauthorized access.

Navigating the Permission Maze

By understanding these potential pitfalls and adopting secure scripting practices, you can navigate the permission maze with confidence, ensuring that your scripts operate safely and responsibly.

3. Checking Permissions – Verifying Access Rights

Before your script attempts to access or modify a file, it's essential to verify that it has the necessary permissions. This prevents errors and ensures that your script operates safely and predictably.

Testing with test or [[ ]]

The `test` command and its equivalent `[[ ]]` syntax, as we learned in Chapter 14, provide various tests for checking file permissions and ownership:

- `-e filename`: Checks if the file exists.
- `-f filename`: Checks if the file is a regular file (not a directory or special file).
- `-d filename`: Checks if the file is a directory.
- `-r filename`: Checks if the file is readable by the current user.
- `-w filename`: Checks if the file is writable by the current user.
- `-x filename`: Checks if the file is executable by the current user.

Example: Verifying File Access

```
filename="data.txt"

if [ -f "$filename" ]; then
  if [ -r "$filename" ]; then
    echo "File '$filename' exists and is readable."
    # Process the file
  else
    echo "File '$filename' exists but is not readable."
    exit 1
  fi
else
  echo "File '$filename' does not exist."
  exit 1
fi
```

This script demonstrates using **test** to verify that the file *data.txt* exists and is readable before attempting to process it. If either condition fails, the script exits with an error message.

Checking Ownership

You can also check the owner and group owner of a file using **test** or **[[ ]]**:
- **-O filename**: Checks if the current user is the owner of the file.
- **-G filename**: Checks if the file's group owner matches the current user's primary group.

For example, to ensure that a script can only be executed by its owner:

```
if [ ! -O "$0" ]; then
  echo "Error: You must be the owner of this script to run it."
  exit 1
fi
```

Verifying Before Acting

By checking permissions and ownership before performing actions, you ensure that your scripts operate safely, avoid errors, and protect your files and system from unauthorized access.

4. Changing Permissions – Modifying Access Control

Sometimes, your script might need to modify file permissions dynamically to accommodate specific tasks or adjust access control during execution. The `chmod` command, as we explored in Chapter 6, provides the tools for changing file modes and adjusting permission bits.

chmod within Scripts

You can use `chmod` within your scripts to modify file permissions as needed. For example, to make a file writable by the owner only:

```
chmod 600 sensitive_data.txt
```

Or, to make a script executable by everyone:

```
chmod +x myscript.sh
```

Choosing Appropriate Permissions

When using `chmod` within your scripts, it's crucial to carefully consider the appropriate permission modes based on the script's requirements and security considerations:
*   **Principle of Least Privilege**: Grant only the minimum permissions necessary for the script to perform its task.
*   **File Ownership**: Ensure that files and directories are owned by the appropriate user and group.
*   **Sensitive Data**: Restrict access to files containing sensitive data by limiting permissions and using appropriate ownership settings.

Dynamic Permission Control

Here are a few scenarios where changing permissions within a script might be necessary:

- **Creating temporary files**: A script might create temporary files during its execution and then remove them before exiting. Setting appropriate permissions on these temporary files can prevent unauthorized access to their contents.
- **Downloading files**: If a script downloads files from the internet, it might need to adjust permissions to make them readable or writable by the user.
- **Generating reports or logs**: A script that generates reports or logs might need to ensure that the output files have appropriate permissions for viewing or sharing.

Modifying Access Dynamically

By using `chmod` effectively within your scripts, you can dynamically control file permissions, ensuring that your script has the necessary access rights while maintaining security and preventing unauthorized access.

5. Elevating Privileges – Using sudo with Caution

While most scripts operate within the confines of the user's permissions, some tasks require elevated privileges, such as modifying system files or performing administrative actions. The `sudo` command, short for "superuser do", provides a mechanism for temporarily elevating privileges to execute commands as another user, typically the superuser (root).

The Power of sudo

The `sudo` command allows authorized users to run commands with the privileges of another user, specified by the command's first argument. For example, to edit the system configuration file */etc/fstab* as the root user:

```
sudo vim /etc/fstab
```

This command will prompt you for your password and, upon successful authentication, will launch the *vim* editor with root privileges, allowing you to modify the file.

sudo in Scripts – A Security Balancing Act

Using sudo within scripts requires careful consideration:
- **Security Implications**: Granting a script blanket sudo privileges can be risky, as it allows the script to perform any action with root permissions, potentially leading to system instability or security breaches if the script is compromised or contains errors.
- **Principle of Least Privilege**: Adhere to the principle of least privilege by using sudo only for specific commands within the script that require elevated privileges, minimizing the potential attack surface.

Configuring sudo

The */etc/sudoers* file controls which users are allowed to execute which commands with sudo. The system administrator can configure this file to grant specific users or groups permission to run certain commands with elevated privileges.

For example, to allow the user "noah" to run the apt-get update and apt-get upgrade commands with sudo:

```
noah ALL=(ALL) NOPASSWD: /usr/bin/apt-get update, /usr/bin/apt-get upgrade
```

This entry in */etc/sudoers* allows "noah" to execute these specific commands without being prompted for a password.

sudo with Discretion

The sudo command is a powerful tool for granting elevated privileges, but it should be used with caution and discretion. By carefully considering the security implications and adhering to best practices, you can leverage sudo to perform necessary tasks within your scripts while maintaining a secure and controlled environment.

6. Best Practices – Securing Your Scripts

Security should be a paramount concern when writing and executing shell scripts, as even a small oversight can have significant consequences. By adopting best practices and following the principle of least privilege, you can ensure that your scripts operate securely and responsibly.

Permission Prudence

- **Follow the Principle of Least Privilege**: Grant your scripts only the minimum permissions necessary to perform their intended tasks. Avoid running scripts with superuser privileges unless absolutely required.
- **Use `sudo` Sparingly**: If elevated privileges are necessary, use `sudo` only for specific commands within the script, rather than granting blanket `sudo` access to the entire script.
- **Validate User Input**: Always validate any user-provided input to prevent malicious code injection or unauthorized access to files and systems.
- **Protect Sensitive Data**: Avoid storing sensitive information, such as passwords or API keys, directly in your scripts. Consider using environment variables or secure storage mechanisms for such data.
- **Be Mindful of File Ownership**: Ensure that script files and the data they access are owned by the appropriate user and group. Avoid using world-writable permissions for scripts or sensitive data.

Scripting with Security in Mind

- **Use a Linter**: Consider using a shell script linter, such as ShellCheck, to identify potential errors and security vulnerabilities in your code.
- **Test Thoroughly**: Test your scripts with various inputs and scenarios to ensure they behave as expected and don't have any unintended side effects.
- **Keep Scripts Updated**: Regularly review and update your scripts to address any security vulnerabilities or incorporate best practices.

A Secure Scripting Environment

By following these best practices and embracing a security-conscious mindset, you can create a more secure scripting environment, protect your data and systems, and ensure that your scripts operate responsibly and reliably.

Chapter Summary

In this chapter, we've delved into the crucial realm of permissions and explored techniques for handling them programmatically within our shell scripts:

- We reviewed the importance of file permissions and ownership, understanding how scripts inherit these attributes from the executing user and the potential security risks associated with excessive permissions.

- We explored common scenarios where script permissions can lead to issues, such as accessing restricted files or modifying system files, and discussed strategies for handling these situations.
- We learned how to check permissions using `test` or `[[ ]]`, verifying access rights before performing actions to prevent errors and ensure script safety.
- We reviewed the `chmod` command and demonstrated its use within scripts for dynamically modifying file permissions.
- We explored the `sudo` command for elevating privileges and discussed best practices for using it cautiously and securely within scripts.
- We embraced security best practices, such as following the principle of least privilege, validating user input, protecting sensitive data, and being mindful of file ownership and permissions.

Remember, handling permissions carefully is essential for creating secure and reliable shell scripts. By applying the principles and techniques covered in this chapter, you can ensure that your scripts operate responsibly, protecting your data and systems from unauthorized access and potential harm.

With a solid understanding of permission management, you're now ready to explore advanced scripting techniques in the next chapter, where we'll delve into the world of functions, local variables, and signal handling to create even more powerful and robust scripts.

Chapter 18:
Advanced Scripting Techniques

While the basic building blocks of scripting provide a solid foundation for creating functional programs, the world of shell scripting extends far beyond simple commands and variables. Like a master craftsman who utilizes specialized tools and techniques to create intricate works of art, advanced scripting concepts allow you to build more complex, modular, and robust scripts.

In this chapter, we'll explore these advanced techniques, delving into the world of functions, local variables, signal handling, and other powerful scripting concepts. You'll learn to create reusable code modules, manage variables with precision, and handle unexpected events with grace and control. Get ready to expand your scripting horizons and elevate your skills to the level of a true scripting virtuoso!

1. Beyond the Basics – Advanced Scripting Horizons

As your scripting journey progresses, you'll encounter scenarios where basic commands and variables alone are not sufficient to tackle the complexities of the task at hand. Imagine constructing a skyscraper using only bricks and mortar – the structure would lack organization, efficiency, and the ability to adapt to changing requirements. Similarly, as your scripts grow in size and complexity, you'll need advanced techniques to build more robust, modular, and maintainable code.

The Challenges of Large Scripts

Large scripts can quickly become unwieldy and difficult to manage, leading to challenges such as:

- **Code Duplication**: Repeating the same blocks of code in multiple places makes the script longer, harder to read, and more prone to errors.
- **Variable Conflicts**: Using the same variable names for different purposes within a script can lead to confusion and unexpected behavior.
- **Lack of Modularity**: Without a clear structure and organization, it becomes difficult to understand the flow of the script and make modifications or enhancements.
- **Error Handling**: Large scripts require robust error handling mechanisms to gracefully handle unexpected situations and prevent failures.

Advanced Techniques to the Rescue

To overcome these challenges, shell scripting offers a range of advanced techniques that elevate your scripts to a new level of sophistication:

- **Shell Functions**: Functions allow you to encapsulate reusable blocks of code into modular units, reducing code duplication and improving organization.
- **Local Variables**: Local variables within functions provide isolated scopes, preventing naming conflicts and enhancing code clarity.
- **Signal Handling**: Signal handling mechanisms enable your scripts to respond to external events and signals, such as user interrupts or termination requests, ensuring graceful exit and cleanup procedures.
- **Process Substitution**: This technique allows you to treat the output of a command as if it were a file, providing greater flexibility in data processing.
- **Asynchronous Execution**: By running commands asynchronously, you can execute multiple processes simultaneously, improving script efficiency and responsiveness.

- **Named Pipes**: Named pipes create communication channels between processes, enabling your scripts to interact with other programs and exchange data.

Expanding Your Scripting Horizons

These advanced techniques empower you to build more complex, modular, and robust scripts, transforming you from a novice scripter into a master craftsman of the command line. In the following sections, we'll explore each of these techniques in detail, unlocking their power and discovering how they can elevate your scripting skills to new heights.

2. Shell Functions – Building Blocks of Code

Imagine constructing a building with prefabricated modules, each serving a specific purpose and easily assembled into a larger structure. **Shell functions** provide a similar modularity for your scripts, allowing you to encapsulate reusable blocks of code into self-contained units.

Defining and Calling Functions

Shell functions are defined using the following syntax:

```
function_name () {
  # commands to be executed
}
```

For example, let's define a function that prints a greeting message:

```
greet () {
  echo "Hello, $1!"
}
```

This function takes one argument (**$1**), which represents the name of the person to greet, and displays a personalized message.

To call a function, simply use its name followed by any arguments:

```
greet "Noah"  # Output: Hello, Noah!
greet "Alice" # Output: Hello, Alice!
```

Function Arguments and Return Values

Functions can accept arguments, which are values passed to the function when it's called. These arguments are accessed within the function using positional parameters ($1, $2, etc.).

Functions can also return values using the `return` command. The return value is an integer representing the exit status of the function. By convention, a return value of 0 indicates success, while non-zero values indicate errors or specific conditions.

Benefits of Using Functions

Shell functions offer several advantages:
- **Code Reusability**: Functions promote code reusability by allowing you to define a block of code once and then call it multiple times from different parts of your script. This reduces code duplication and makes your scripts more concise and maintainable.
- **Modularity**: Functions break down complex tasks into smaller, self-contained units, improving the organization and structure of your scripts.
- **Readability**: By giving functions descriptive names, you can improve the readability of your code and make it easier to understand the overall flow of the script.

Building with Functions

Shell functions are essential building blocks for creating well-structured, modular, and reusable scripts. By mastering the art of defining and utilizing functions, you'll enhance the efficiency, maintainability, and readability of your scripting projects.

3. Local Variables – Function Scope

Imagine a construction crew working on a specific section of a building, using tools and materials that are dedicated to that area and don't interfere with the work happening in other parts of the building. **Local variables** in shell functions provide a similar isolation, creating variables that exist only within the scope of the function and don't affect the global script environment.

Declaring Local Variables

To create a local variable within a function, you use the `local` keyword:

```
function_name () {
  local variable_name=value
  # ...
}
```

For example:

```
greet () {
  local message="Hello, $1!"
  echo "$message"
}
```

In this example, the variable *message* is declared as a local variable within the *greet* function. Its scope is limited to the function, and it will not be accessible outside of the function's code block.

Global vs. Local – Understanding Scope

- **Global variables**: Variables declared outside of any function are global variables. They are accessible from anywhere within the script, including inside functions.
- **Local variables**: Variables declared with the `local` keyword within a function are local to that function. They are not accessible outside of the function's scope.

Benefits of Local Variables

Using local variables offers several advantages:
- **Preventing Naming Conflicts**: Local variables avoid conflicts with global variables that might have the same name. This allows you to use meaningful variable names within functions without worrying about interfering with variables used elsewhere in the script.
- **Improved Modularity**: Local variables enhance the modularity of your functions by isolating their internal data from the global environment. This makes functions more self-contained and easier to reuse in different contexts.

- **Cleaner Code**: By using local variables, you reduce the clutter of global variables and make your code easier to read and understand.

Localizing Your Data

Local variables provide a mechanism for creating isolated data environments within your shell functions, enhancing code clarity, modularity, and maintainability. By understanding the scope of variables and using local variables effectively, you'll build more robust and well-structured scripts.

4. Signal Handling – Responding to Events

Imagine a fire alarm system that triggers a series of actions when it detects smoke or heat. **Signal handling** in shell scripts provides a similar mechanism for responding to external events and signals, allowing your scripts to react gracefully to unexpected situations and perform necessary cleanup tasks before exiting.

Traps – Catching Signals

The `trap` command is your tool for setting up **signal handlers**, which are routines that are executed when a specific signal is received by the script. The basic syntax is:

```
trap command signals
```

- `command`: The command or function to be executed when the signal is received.
- `signals`: One or more signal names or numbers.

Common Signals

Here are a few commonly handled signals:
- `SIGINT` **(interrupt)**: This signal is sent when the user presses `Ctrl+C`, typically used to interrupt a running program.
- `SIGTERM` **(termination)**: This signal is sent to request the termination of a process. It's often used by system administrators to gracefully shut down services or processes.
- `SIGKILL` **(kill)**: This signal forcefully terminates a process and cannot be caught or ignored.
- `SIGHUP` **(hangup)**: This signal is sent when the controlling terminal is closed or the connection is lost.

Example: Handling Interrupts

```
Cleanup () {
    echo "Cleaning up temporary files ..."
    rm -f /tmp/mytempfile.txt
    exit 0
}


trap cleanup SIGINT


# ... rest of the script ...
```

This script defines a function named `cleanup` that removes a temporary file and exits gracefully. The `trap` command then sets up a signal handler for SIGINT, which will execute the `cleanup` function if the user presses Ctrl+C during the script's execution.

Graceful Exits and Cleanup

Signal handling is essential for creating robust and reliable scripts. It allows you to:
- **Clean up temporary files**: Ensure that temporary files or resources are properly cleaned up before the script exits, preventing clutter and potential data leaks.
- **Save progress**: In certain cases, you might want to save the script's progress or state before exiting, allowing for resuming later.
- **Exit gracefully**: Provide informative messages or perform necessary actions before terminating the script.

Responding to the Unexpected

By mastering the art of signal handling, you empower your scripts to respond intelligently to unexpected events and ensure their proper and orderly termination, even in the face of interruptions or system shutdowns.

5. Process Substitution – File-Like Magic

Imagine having the ability to conjure a temporary file containing the output of a command, allowing you to use that output as input for another command without actually creating a physical file on disk. **Process substitution** provides this magical

206

ability, creating a virtual file that represents the output of a process and can be used as input for other commands.

The Illusion of Files

Process substitution uses the following syntax:
- `<(...)`: Captures the standard output (stdout) of a command and creates a virtual file that can be used as input for another command.
- `>(...)`: Captures the standard input (stdin) of a command and creates a virtual file that can be written to.

These constructs create temporary files in the */dev/fd* directory, which are then automatically deleted when the command finishes executing.

Examples of Process Substitution

Here are a few examples of how process substitution can be used:
- Comparing the output of two commands:

```
diff <(ls -l dir1) <(ls -l dir2)
```

This command compares the directory listings of *dir1* and *dir2* using `diff`, treating the output of each `ls -l` command as a virtual file.
- Sorting the output of a command:

```
sort <(ps aux | grep "process_name")
```

This command sorts the output of the `ps aux | grep "process_name"` pipeline, treating the filtered process list as a virtual file.
- Passing data to a command that expects a filename:

```
grep "pattern" > >(tee matched_lines.txt | wc -1)
```

This command searches for "pattern" in the input and writes the matching lines to a virtual file. The virtual file is then piped to `tee`, which both saves the lines to *matched_lines.txt* and pipes them to `wc -1` to count the number of matches.

The Power of Illusion

Process substitution provides a powerful and efficient way to use the output of one command as input for another, without the need to create intermediate temporary files. It streamlines data processing and allows for more concise and elegant command-line operations.

6. Asynchronous Execution – Parallel Processing

Imagine a team of workers collaborating on a project, each performing their tasks concurrently, rather than waiting for one another to finish. **Asynchronous execution** in shell scripting allows you to achieve a similar parallelism, running multiple processes simultaneously and improving the efficiency and responsiveness of your scripts.

Running Commands in the Background

To execute a command asynchronously, you can append an ampersand (**&**) to the end of the command line:

```
command &
```

This will launch the command in the background, allowing your script to continue executing other commands without waiting for the background process to finish.

For example:

```
wget https://example.com/large_file.zip &
echo "Download started in the background..."
# ... other commands ...
```

This script starts a download in the background using **wget** and then immediately displays a message and continues with other tasks, without waiting for the download to complete.

Waiting for Background Processes

To synchronize your script's execution and ensure that background processes have completed before proceeding, you can use the **wait** command:

```
wait [job_id ...]
```

- **[job_id ...]** (optional): Specifies one or more job IDs (process IDs) to wait for. If no job IDs are provided, **wait** will wait for all child processes to complete.

Example: Synchronizing Processes

```
Process1 &
pid1=$!  # Store the process ID of process1
process2 &
pid2=$!  # Store the process ID of process2
wait $pid1 $pid2
echo "Both processes have finished."
```

This script runs *process1* and *process2* in the background, stores their process IDs, and then uses `wait` to pause execution until both processes have completed.

The Efficiency of Parallelism

Asynchronous execution allows your scripts to perform multiple tasks concurrently, improving efficiency and responsiveness. By using background processes and the `wait` command, you can create scripts that handle multiple tasks simultaneously while maintaining control over their execution flow.

7. Named Pipes – Communication Channels

Imagine a pair of walkie-talkies allowing two people to communicate over a distance. **Named pipes** in Linux provide a similar communication channel between processes, enabling them to exchange data and synchronize their actions.

Creating a Named Pipe

To create a named pipe, use the `mkfifo` command:

```
mkfifo pipe_name
```

This command creates a special file with the specified *pipe_name*. This file acts as a FIFO (first-in, first-out) buffer, where data written to one end of the pipe can be read from the other end.

Using Named Pipes

Once a named pipe is created, you can use it to connect two processes:

- **Process 1**: Writes data to the pipe using redirection (>).
- **Process 2**: Reads data from the pipe using redirection (<).

For example:

```
# Terminal 1
mkfifo mypipe
echo "This is a message." > mypipe


# Terminal 2
cat < mypipe
```

In this example, the first terminal creates a named pipe called *mypipe* and writes a message to it. The second terminal reads from the pipe and displays the message.

Inter-Process Communication

Named pipes are valuable tools for inter-process communication, enabling you to:
- **Connect scripts with other programs**: A script can send data to another program or receive data from it using a named pipe.
- **Create producer-consumer workflows**: One process can act as a producer, generating data and writing it to the pipe, while another process acts as a consumer, reading and processing the data from the pipe.
- **Synchronize processes**: Processes can use named pipes to signal each other and coordinate their actions.

Communication Channels for Collaboration

Named pipes provide a flexible and efficient way for processes to communicate and collaborate, enabling you to create complex workflows and interactions between your scripts and other programs.

Chapter Summary

In this chapter, we've ventured beyond the basics of scripting and explored advanced techniques that empower us to build more sophisticated and robust programs:
- We recognized the challenges of managing large scripts and the need for modularity, organization, and efficient data processing.

- We learned how to create and utilize **shell functions** as reusable building blocks of code, promoting code organization, reducing duplication, and improving readability.
- We explored the concept of **local variables** and their scope within functions, understanding how they prevent naming conflicts and enhance code modularity.
- We mastered the art of **signal handling** with `trap`, enabling our scripts to respond gracefully to external events and signals, perform cleanup tasks, and exit cleanly.
- We discovered the magic of **process substitution**, creating virtual files from the output of commands and streamlining data processing.
- We explored **asynchronous execution** using background processes and the `wait` command, allowing our scripts to perform multiple tasks concurrently and improve efficiency.
- We delved into **named pipes** as communication channels between processes, enabling inter-process collaboration and data exchange.

These advanced techniques provide a powerful toolkit for building complex, modular, and reliable scripts. By mastering these concepts and applying them creatively, you'll elevate your scripting skills and create programs that are well-structured, efficient, and capable of handling a wide range of challenges.

With these advanced techniques under your belt, you're now well-equipped to tackle the final chapter, where we'll explore the art of debugging and troubleshooting, ensuring that your scripts run smoothly and behave as intended.

Chapter 19:
Debugging and
Troubleshooting

Even the most seasoned shell scripting wizards encounter glitches and gremlins in their code. Bugs are an inevitable part of the programming journey, and the ability to identify, isolate, and exterminate them is a crucial skill for any aspiring scripter.

In this chapter, we'll embark on a quest of **debugging and troubleshooting**, learning to become adept bug hunters and problem solvers. We'll explore common types of errors, discover techniques for identifying the source of problems, and adopt defensive programming strategies to prevent bugs from creeping into our code. So, grab your metaphorical magnifying glass and prepare to delve into the world of script debugging!

1. Debugging – The Art of Bug Hunting

Debugging is the process of identifying, isolating, and fixing errors, or bugs, in your scripts. It's an essential skill for any programmer, as even small errors can cause unexpected behavior, incorrect results, or complete script failures.

The Debugging Mindset

Debugging requires a combination of analytical thinking, problem-solving skills, and a healthy dose of patience. It's like being a detective, searching for clues, piecing together evidence, and ultimately uncovering the culprit behind the script's misbehavior.

Here are some key aspects of effective debugging:
*   **Understanding the Problem**: Clearly define the issue you're experiencing. What is the script supposed to do, and how is it behaving instead? Gathering specific details about the error or unexpected behavior will help you narrow down the search for the bug.
*   **Methodical Approach**: Don't blindly change code and hope for the best. Use a systematic approach to identify the source of the problem, such as tracing the script's execution or examining variable values at different points.
*   **Divide and Conquer**: Break down the script into smaller sections and test them individually to isolate the problematic area. This can help you narrow down the search and focus on the specific code that's causing the issue.
*   **Experimentation**: Don't be afraid to try different solutions and experiment with various approaches to fix the bug. Sometimes, a creative approach or a fresh perspective can lead to the breakthrough you need.
*   **Seeking Help**: When you're stuck, don't hesitate to seek help from online resources, communities, or experienced programmers. Often, a second pair of eyes or a different perspective can provide the insight you need to solve the problem.

The Rewards of Bug Hunting

Debugging can be a challenging and sometimes frustrating process, but it's also incredibly rewarding. When you finally track down and fix a bug, you not only improve the functionality and reliability of your script, but you also gain valuable knowledge and experience that will make you a better scripter in the long run.

2. Types of Errors – Syntax vs. Logic

Bugs can manifest in various forms, but they generally fall into two main categories: **syntax errors** and **logical errors**. Understanding the difference between these types of errors is crucial for effective debugging, as they require different approaches to identify and fix.

Syntax Errors – The Grammar Police

Syntax errors are like grammatical mistakes in a sentence – they violate the rules of the shell's language, preventing the script from being understood and executed correctly. The shell will typically detect syntax errors and display an error message indicating the line number and the nature of the problem.

Here are some common examples of syntax errors:

- **Missing or mismatched quotes**: Forgetting to close a string with quotes or using mismatched quotes (e.g., starting with a double quote and ending with a single quote) can confuse the shell and lead to errors.
- **Unclosed loops or conditional statements**: Forgetting to include the closing keywords `fi`, `done`, or `esac` for `if` statements, loops, or `case` statements, respectively, will result in a syntax error.
- **Missing semicolons**: Semicolons are used to separate commands on the same line. Omitting a semicolon can cause the shell to misinterpret the commands and generate an error.
- **Misspelled commands or keywords**: Typos in command names or keywords (e.g., `if`, `then`, `else`) will prevent the shell from recognizing them, leading to syntax errors.

Logical Errors – The Silent Culprits

Logical errors are more insidious, as they don't prevent the script from running, but they cause it to produce incorrect results or behave unexpectedly. These errors are like faulty reasoning in a detective's investigation, leading them down the wrong path.

Here are some examples of logical errors:

- **Incorrect conditional expressions**: Using the wrong comparison operator (e.g., using = instead of == for string comparisons) or misinterpreting the logic of a condition can lead to unexpected results.
- **Off-by-one errors**: Mistakes in loop counters or array indices, such as starting from the wrong index or iterating one too many times, can cause the script to process data incorrectly.

- **Unhandled edge cases**: Failing to consider all possible input values or scenarios can lead to unexpected behavior when the script encounters edge cases or unusual data.

Identifying the Culprits

Syntax errors are usually easier to spot due to the helpful error messages provided by the shell. Logical errors, on the other hand, require more detective work, as you need to analyze the script's behavior, trace its execution, and examine variable values to identify the source of the problem.

In the following sections, we'll explore various techniques for identifying and isolating both types of errors, equipping you with the tools to become an effective bug hunter.

3. Identifying Errors – Detective Work

Tracking down bugs in your scripts requires a keen eye for detail and a methodical approach. Like a detective examining a crime scene, you need to gather evidence, analyze clues, and follow leads to uncover the culprit behind the script's misbehavior.

Error Messages – The Initial Clues

When your script encounters a syntax error, the shell will usually display an error message indicating the line number and the nature of the problem. These messages are your first clues, providing valuable information about the location and type of error.

For example, an error message like:

```
line 5: syntax error near unexpected token `fi'
```

tells you that there's a syntax error on line 5 near the `fi` keyword, suggesting that you might have an unclosed `if` statement or a misplaced `fi`.

Script Tracing – Following the Execution Path

To observe the flow of execution within your script and identify potential logical errors, you can use the `set -x` option. This enables **script tracing**, which causes the shell to print each command and its arguments before executing them.

```
#!/bin/bash -x

# ... script code ...
```

Adding -x to the shebang line enables tracing for the entire script. You can also use set -x and set +x to turn tracing on and off within specific sections of the script.

The PS4 variable controls the format of the trace output. By default, it displays a + symbol before each traced line. You can customize this to include more informative details, such as line numbers:

```
export PS4='+(${LINENO}): '
```

Echo Statements – Revealing Variable Values

Inserting echo statements at various points in your script can help you track down logical errors by displaying the values of variables or indicating the progress of the script's execution.

For example:

```
echo "Variable value: $variable"
echo "Reached this point in the script."
```

Commenting Out Code – Isolating Problems

If you suspect a particular section of code is causing issues, you can temporarily comment out that section using the # symbol at the beginning of each line. This prevents the code from being executed, allowing you to test the rest of the script and see if the error persists.

Gathering the Evidence

By utilizing these debugging techniques, you can gather evidence about your script's behavior, identify the source of errors, and begin the process of fixing them.

4. Defensive Programming – Preventing Errors

Debugging is essential for fixing errors, but preventing them in the first place is even better! **Defensive programming** is a mindset and a set of techniques that aim to

216

minimize the likelihood of errors occurring in your scripts, making them more robust, reliable, and easier to maintain.

Input Validation – Trust No One

One of the most common sources of errors is unexpected or invalid user input. Always validate any data that your script receives from the user, ensuring it meets the expected format and criteria.

For example, if your script expects a number, check if the user input is actually a number:

```
read -p "Enter a number: " number

if [[ ! "$number" =~ ^[0-9]+$ ]]; then
  echo "Error: Invalid input. Please enter a number."
  exit 1
fi
```

This code snippet uses a regular expression to validate that the input consists only of digits.

Condition Checking – Anticipate the Unexpected

Anticipate potential errors by checking for expected conditions before performing actions. For example, if your script attempts to read a file, ensure the file exists and is readable:

```
if [[ -f "$filename" && -r "$filename" ]]; then
  # Read the file
else
  echo "Error: Cannot access file '$filename'."
  exit 1
fi
```

The Power of set -e

The set -e option instructs the shell to exit immediately if any command within the script returns a non-zero exit status, indicating an error. This prevents errors from cascading and potentially causing further damage or unexpected behavior.

```
#!/bin/bash -e

# ... script code ...
```

Use `set -e` with caution, as it might terminate the script prematurely in situations where you want to handle errors gracefully or continue execution despite non-critical errors.

Error Handling with `trap`

As we learned in the previous chapter, the `trap` command allows you to set up signal handlers for specific signals, such as `SIGINT` (Ctrl+C) or `SIGTERM`. You can use `trap` to implement error handling routines that perform cleanup tasks or display informative messages when errors occur.

For example:

```
error_handler () {
    echo "An error occurred. Exiting."
    exit 1
}


trap error_handler ERR
```

This code snippet defines an *error_handler* function and sets up a trap for the `ERR` signal, which is triggered when a command returns a non-zero exit status.

Defensive Programming Mindset

By adopting a defensive programming mindset and implementing techniques for input validation, condition checking, error handling, and utilizing options like `set -e`, you can significantly reduce the likelihood of errors occurring in your scripts, making them more robust, reliable, and easier to maintain.

5. Debugging Tips and Strategies

Debugging is both an art and a science, requiring a combination of logic, intuition, and a systematic approach. Here are some practical tips and strategies to enhance your debugging skills and make the bug-hunting process more efficient and less frustrating:

Understand the Problem

Before you dive into debugging, clearly define the issue you're experiencing. What is the script supposed to do, and how is it behaving differently? Gather as much information as possible about the error or unexpected behavior:

- **Error messages**: Carefully read and analyze the error messages provided by the shell. They often contain valuable clues about the location and nature of the problem.
- **Input values**: Note the specific input values that trigger the error.
- **Expected output**: Determine what the expected output should be and how it differs from the actual output.

Divide and Conquer

Break down your script into smaller, manageable sections and test each section independently. This helps you isolate the problematic area and narrow down the search for the bug. You can use commenting out code or inserting `echo` statements to track the flow of execution and identify the point where the error occurs.

Use Tracing Effectively

Script tracing with `set -x` is a powerful tool, but it can produce a lot of output, making it difficult to analyze. Focus your tracing on specific sections of code where you suspect the error lies, or customize the `PS4` variable to display only the information you need, such as line numbers or variable values.

Examine Variable Values

Logical errors often stem from incorrect variable values or unexpected data transformations. Use `echo` statements to display the values of relevant variables at different points in your script, helping you track down the source of the problem.

Test with Different Inputs

Test your script with various inputs and scenarios, including edge cases and boundary conditions. This helps you uncover hidden bugs and ensures that your script behaves correctly under a range of circumstances.

Seek Help When Needed

Don't be afraid to ask for help! Online resources, forums, and communities like Stack Overflow and LinuxQuestions.org are invaluable for finding solutions to common problems, getting advice from experienced scripters, and gaining new perspectives on your debugging challenges.

The Debugging Journey

Debugging is a continuous learning process. As you encounter different types of errors and solve challenging bugs, you'll develop your debugging skills, gain a deeper understanding of shell scripting, and become a more confident and effective programmer.

Remember, patience, persistence, and a methodical approach are your allies in the bug-hunting quest!

Chapter Summary

In this chapter, we've journeyed into the world of debugging and troubleshooting, acquiring the skills and mindset of a seasoned bug hunter:

- We emphasized the importance of debugging in script development, understanding that even small errors can have significant consequences for a script's functionality and reliability.
- We distinguished between the two main types of errors – syntax errors and logical errors – recognizing their unique characteristics and the different approaches required to identify and fix them.
- We explored various techniques for identifying errors, including analyzing error messages, tracing script execution with `set -x`, inserting `echo` statements to reveal variable values, and commenting out code to isolate problematic areas.
- We embraced the concept of defensive programming, learning how to prevent errors by validating user input, checking for expected conditions, using the `set -e` option to terminate on errors, and implementing error handling routines with `trap`.
- We shared practical tips and strategies for effective debugging, emphasizing a methodical approach, experimentation, and the value of seeking help when needed.

Debugging is an essential skill for any shell scripter, and it's a skill that develops through practice and perseverance. By mastering the techniques and strategies

220

covered in this chapter, you'll be well-equipped to track down and exterminate bugs, creating scripts that are robust, reliable, and ready to tackle any challenge.

With your newfound debugging expertise, you're now prepared to embark on your own scripting adventures, confidently creating and maintaining scripts that automate tasks, process data, and unlock the full potential of the Linux command line.

Appendix A: Command Reference

1. File and Directory Management

This section provides a quick reference for commands used to manage files and directories, including navigating the file system, creating and deleting files and directories, copying and moving files, and working with links.

Command	Description
pwd	• **Purpose**: Displays the current working directory, showing your location in the file system. • **Syntax**: **pwd** • **Options**: None • **Reference**: Chapter 1
cd	• **Purpose**: Changes the current working directory, allowing you to navigate to different locations in the file system. • **Syntax**: **cd [directory]** • **Common Options**: ○ **cd (no arguments)**: Changes to the user's home directory. ○ **cd -**: Changes to the previous working directory. • **Reference**: Chapter 1

ls	• **Purpose**: Lists the contents of directories, displaying files and subdirectories.
	• **Syntax: ls [options] [directory...]**
	• **Common Options**:
	  ○ **-l**: Displays a long listing format, showing detailed information about each file and directory, including permissions, ownership, size, and modification date.
	  ○ **-a**: Lists all files, including hidden files (those starting with a dot).
	  ○ **-h**: When used with **-l**, displays file sizes in a human-readable format (KB, MB, GB).
	  ○ **-R**: Lists files and directories recursively, descending into subdirectories.
	  ○ **-t**: Sorts by modification time, showing the most recently modified files first.
	  ○ **-S**: Sorts by file size, showing the largest files first.
	  ○ **-r**: Reverses the order of the sort.
	• **Reference**: Chapter 1, 2, 8

mkdir	• **Purpose**: Creates new directories. • **Syntax: mkdir [options] directory...** • **Common Options**: ○ **-p**: Creates parent directories as needed, allowing you to create a nested directory structure with a single command. • **Reference**: Chapter 2

touch	• **Purpose**: Creates empty files or updates file timestamps.
	• **Syntax: touch [options] file...**
	• **Common Options**:
	  ○ **-a**: Updates only the access time.
	  ○ **-m**: Updates only the modification time.
	• **Reference**: Chapter 2

cp	• **Purpose**: Copies files and directories.
	• **Syntax: cp [options] source destination**
	• **Common Options**:
	  ○ **-i**: Prompts before overwriting existing files.
	  ○ **-r**: Copies directories recursively, including their contents.
	• **Reference**: Chapter 2

mv	• **Purpose**: Moves or renames files and directories. • **Syntax: mv [options] source destination** • **Common Options**: ○ **-i**: Prompts before overwriting existing files. • **Reference**: Chapter 2

rm	• **Purpose**: Removes (deletes) files and directories.
	• **Syntax: rm [options] file...**
	• **Common Options**:
	  ○ **-i**: Prompts before deleting files.
	  ○ **-r**: Deletes directories recursively.
	  ○ **-f**: Forces deletion without prompting, even for protected files. Use with extreme caution!
	• **Reference**: Chapter 2

ln	• **Purpose**: Creates links, either hard links or symbolic links.
	• **Syntax**:
	  ○ **Hard link: ln target_file link_name**
	  ○ **Symbolic link: ln -s target_file link_name**
	• **Reference**: Chapter 3

find	• **Purpose**: Searches for files in a directory hierarchy based on various criteria. • **Syntax: find [starting_directory...] [expression]** • **Common Options**: ○ Refer to the **man** page for **find** (Chapter 17) for a comprehensive list of tests, actions, and options. • **Reference**: Chapter 17
locate	• **Purpose**: Finds files by name using a database of file locations. • **Syntax: locate [options] pattern** • **Reference**: Chapter 17

2. Text Processing

This section provides a quick reference for commands used to process and manipulate text data, including viewing, searching, sorting, filtering, transforming, and comparing text files.

Command	Description

cat	• **Purpose**: Concatenates and displays the contents of files or standard input.
	• **Syntax: cat [options] [file...]**
	• **Common Options:**
	  ○ **-n**: Numbers all output lines.
	  ○ **-s**: Suppresses repeated empty output lines.
	  ○ **-A**: Displays non-printing characters (tabs, spaces) using control characters (e.g., ^I for tab, $ for end of line).
	• **Reference**: Chapters 5, 6, 7

echo	• **Purpose**: Displays text or the value of a variable.
	• **Syntax: echo [options] [string...]**
	• **Common Options:**
	  ○ **-n**: Suppresses the trailing newline, allowing you to print text on the same line.
	  ○ **-e**: Enables the interpretation of escape sequences (e.g., \n for newline, \t for tab).
	• **Reference**: Chapter 12

grep	• **Purpose**: Searches text for lines matching a specified pattern using regular expressions.
	• **Syntax: grep [options] pattern [file...]**
	• **Common Options:**
	  ○ **-i**: Performs a case-insensitive search.
	  ○ **-v**: Displays lines that do not match the pattern.
	  ○ **-c**: Prints only the count of matching lines.
	  ○ **-n**: Displays matching lines with their line numbers.
	  ○ **-E**: Uses extended regular expression syntax (ERE).
	• **Reference**: Chapters 7, 10

sort	• **Purpose**: Sorts lines of text files or standard input.
	• **Syntax: sort [options] [file...]**
	• **Common Options:**
	  ◦ **-n**: Sorts numerically.
	  ◦ **-r**: Sorts in reverse order (descending).
	  ◦ **-k field_num**: Sorts based on a specific field (column) within each line.
	  ◦ **-t delimiter**: Specifies the delimiter character used to separate fields.
	• **Reference**: Chapter 7

uniq	• **Purpose**: Removes duplicate lines from sorted input.
	• **Syntax: uniq [options] [input_file]**
	• **Common Options:**
	  ◦ **-c**: Displays each unique line along with the number of times it appeared consecutively in the input.
	  ◦ **-d**: Displays only the lines that have duplicates.
	  ◦ **-u**: Displays only the unique lines, omitting duplicates.
	• **Reference**: Chapter 7

wc	• **Purpose**: Counts lines, words, and bytes in files or standard input.
	• **Syntax: wc [options] [file...]**
	• **Common Options:**
	  ◦ **-l**: Counts only lines.
	  ◦ **-w**: Counts only words.
	  ◦ **-c**: Counts only bytes.
	• **Reference**: Chapter 7

head	• **Purpose**: Displays the beginning lines of a file or standard input. • **Syntax: head [options] [file...]** • **Common Options:** ◦ **-n num**: Displays the first *num* lines. • **Reference**: Chapter 7

tail	• **Purpose**: Displays the ending lines of a file or standard input.
	• **Syntax: tail [options] [file...]**
	• **Common Options:**
	  ◦ **-n num**: Displays the last *num* lines.
	  ◦ **-f**: Follows the file, continuously displaying new lines as they are added (useful for monitoring log files).
	• **Reference**: Chapter 7

cut	• **Purpose**: Extracts specific sections of text from lines, either by character positions or fields.
	• **Syntax: cut [options] [file...]**
	• **Common Options**:
	  ○ **-c list**: Extracts characters specified by *list* (e.g., 1-5,10,20-).
	  ○ **-f list**: Extracts fields (columns) specified by *list* (e.g., 1,3).
	  ○ **-d delimiter**: Specifies the delimiter character used to separate fields.
	• **Reference**: Chapter 8

paste	• **Purpose**: Merges lines from multiple files or standard input, aligning them horizontally.
	• **Syntax: paste [options] file...**
	• **Common Options**:
	  ○ **-d delimiter**: Specifies the delimiter character used to separate fields in the output.
	  ○ **-s**: Merges files serially, placing lines from each file below each other.
	• **Reference**: Chapter 8

join	• **Purpose**: Merges lines from two files based on a common field, similar to a database join operation.
	• **Syntax: join [options] file1 file2**
	• **Common Options**:
	  ○ **-1 field_num**: Specifies the join field number in the first file.
	  ○ **-2 field_num**: Specifies the join field number in the second file.
	  ○ **-t delimiter**: Specifies the field delimiter for both input files.
	  ○ **-o format**: Controls the format of the output, specifying which fields to include.
	• **Reference**: Chapter 8

comm	• **Purpose**: Compares two sorted files line by line, identifying unique and common lines.
	• **Syntax: comm [options] file1 file2**
	• **Common Options**:
	  ○ **-1**: Suppresses the first column (lines unique to file1).
	  ○ **-2**: Suppresses the second column (lines unique to file2).
	  ○ **-3**: Suppresses the third column (common lines).
	• **Reference**: Chapter 9

diff	• **Purpose**: Compares files line by line and displays the differences between them.
	• **Syntax: diff [options] file1 file2**
	• **Common Options**:
	  ○ **-c**: Displays the differences in context format, showing the changed lines along with surrounding context.
	  ○ **-u**: Displays the differences in unified format, which is a more concise version of the context format.
	• **Reference**: Chapter 9

patch	• **Purpose**: Applies changes from a diff file (patch file) to a target file.
	• **Syntax: patch [options] [original_file] < patch_file**
	• **Common Options**:
	  ○ **-p num**: Strips leading components from file paths in the patch file.
	  ○ **-R**: Reverses the patch, undoing the changes.
	• **Reference**: Chapter 9

sed	• **Purpose**: A stream editor for performing non-interactive text manipulations.
	• **Syntax: sed [options] 'command' [input_file...]**
	• **Common Options**:
	  ○ **-i**: Edits files in-place, modifying the original files directly.
	  ○ **-n**: Suppresses automatic printing of lines.
	  ○ **-e command**: Specifies a **sed** command to execute.
	  ○ **-f script_file**: Reads commands from a script file.
	• **Reference**: Chapter 11

tr	• **Purpose**: Translates or deletes characters.
	• **Syntax: tr [options] set1 [set2]**
	• **Common Options**:
	  ○ **-d**: Deletes characters in *set1*.
	  ○ **-s**: Squeezes (removes) repeated characters in *set1*.
	• **Reference**: Chapter 11

3. Permissions and Ownership

This section provides a quick reference for commands related to file permissions and ownership, including modifying permissions, setting default permissions, changing ownership, displaying user identity, and temporarily elevating privileges.

Command	Description

chmod	• **Purpose**: Changes the permissions of files and directories.
	• **Syntax**:
	  ○ **Octal notation: chmod mode file...** (e.g., **chmod 644 myfile.txt**)
	  ○ **Symbolic notation: chmod [ugoa][+-=][rwx] file...** (e.g., **chmod u+x myscript.sh**)
	• **Reference**: Chapters 6, 17

umask	• **Purpose**: Sets the default permissions for newly created files and directories. • **Syntax: umask [mode]** (*mode* is an octal number, e.g., **umask 0002**) • **Reference**: Chapter 6
chown	• **Purpose**: Changes the owner of files and directories. • **Syntax: chown [owner][:group] file...** (e.g., **chown noah:users myfile.txt**) • **Reference**: Chapter 6
chgrp	• **Purpose**: Changes the group owner of files and directories. • **Syntax: chgrp group file...** (e.g., **chgrp project_team project.tgz**) • **Reference**: Chapter 6

id	• **Purpose**: Displays user and group information for the current user.
	• **Syntax**: **id [options]**
	• **Common Options**:
	   ○ **-u**: Displays only the user ID (UID).
	   ○ **-g**: Displays only the group ID (GID).
	   ○ **-G**: Displays all group IDs.
	• **Reference**: Chapter 6

sudo	• **Purpose**: Executes a command as another user, typically the superuser (root). • **Syntax**: **sudo [options] command** • **Reference**: Chapters 6, 17

233

4. Process Management

This section provides a quick reference for commands used to manage processes, including viewing running processes, monitoring system performance, controlling process execution, and sending signals.

Command	Description

ps	• **Purpose**: Displays information about currently running processes.
	• **Syntax: ps [options]**
	• **Common Options:**
	  ○ **-aux**: Displays all processes, including those not associated with a terminal.
	  ○ **-ef**: Displays processes in a full-format listing, similar to **aux**.
	  ○ **-u user**: Displays processes owned by the specified user.
	• **Reference**: Chapter 10

top	• **Purpose**: Displays a dynamic, real-time view of system processes, sorted by CPU usage.
	• **Syntax: top**
	• **Common Interactive Commands:**
	  ○ **h**: Displays the help screen.
	  ○ **q**: Quits **top**.
	• **Reference**: Chapter 10

jobs	• **Purpose**: Lists the jobs (processes) running in the current shell session. • **Syntax: jobs [options]** • **Reference**: Chapter 10

kill	• **Purpose**: Sends a signal to a process, allowing you to terminate or control its execution.
	• **Syntax: kill [signal] pid...**
	• **Common Signals**:
	  ○ **1 (HUP)**: Hang up. Often used to reinitialize daemons or reload configuration files.
	  ○ **2 (INT)**: Interrupt. Typically terminates a process.
	  ○ **9 (KILL)**: Forcefully terminates a process (cannot be caught or ignored).
	  ○ **15 (TERM)**: Termination signal. Requests a process to terminate gracefully.
	• **Reference**: Chapter 10

killall	• **Purpose**: Kills processes by name.
	• **Syntax: killall [options] process_name...**
	• **Common Options**:
	  ○ **-i**: Prompts before killing each process.
	  ○ **-u user**: Kills processes owned by the specified user.
	• **Reference**: Chapter 10

bg	• **Purpose**: Places a suspended job in the background. • **Syntax: bg [jobspec]** ○ **[jobspec] (optional)**: Specifies the job to be placed in the background (e.g., %1, %2). If omitted, the most recently suspended job is used. • **Reference**: Chapter 10
fg	• **Purpose**: Brings a background job to the foreground. • **Syntax: fg [jobspec]** ○ **[jobspec] (optional)**: Specifies the job to be brought to the foreground. If omitted, the most recently backgrounded job is used. • **Reference**: Chapter 10

5. System Information

This section provides a quick reference for commands used to retrieve information about the system, including the current date and time, disk space usage, file sizes, system uptime, and general system details.

Command	Description
date	• **Purpose**: Displays or sets the system date and time. • **Syntax**: ○ **Display date**: **date [format]** (refer to the **man** page for **date** for formatting options) ○ **Set date**: **sudo date [MMDDhhmm[[CC]YY][.ss]]** • **Reference**: Chapter 5
df	• **Purpose**: Displays disk space usage information for file systems. • **Syntax**: **df [options]** • **Common Options**: ○ **-h**: Displays sizes in human-readable format (KB, MB, GB). ○ **-T**: Displays file system types. • **Reference**: Chapter 5
du	• **Purpose**: Estimates file space usage. • **Syntax**: **du [options] [file...]** • **Common Options**: ○ **-h**: Displays sizes in human-readable format. ○ **-s**: Displays only a total for each argument. • **Reference**: Chapter 13
uptime	• **Purpose**: Displays the system uptime (amount of time the system has been running). • **Syntax**: **uptime** • **Reference**: Chapter 13

uname	• **Purpose**: Displays system information, such as the operating system name, kernel version, and hardware architecture.
	• **Syntax**: **uname [options]**
	• **Common Options**:
	  ○ **-a**: Displays all available system information.
	  ○ **-s**: Displays the kernel name.
	  ○ **-r**: Displays the kernel release.
	  ○ **-m**: Displays the hardware name.
	• Reference: Chapter 13

6. Other Utilities

This section provides a quick reference for various utility commands that don't fit neatly into other categories, including commands for managing the terminal, accessing documentation, creating aliases, and viewing command history.

Command	Description
clear	• **Purpose**: Clears the terminal screen. • **Syntax**: **clear** • **Reference**: Chapter 1
man	• **Purpose**: Displays manual pages for commands, utilities, system calls, and other topics. • **Syntax**: **man [section] command** • **Common Options**: ○ **-k keyword or apropos keyword**: Searches for manual pages containing the keyword in their description. • **Reference**: Chapter 4
info	• **Purpose**: Displays GNU Info pages, providing comprehensive documentation for GNU programs. • **Syntax**: **info [topic]** • **Reference**: Chapter 4
apropos	• **Purpose**: Searches for manual pages containing a keyword in their description. • **Syntax**: **apropos keyword** • **Reference**: Chapter 4
whatis	• **Purpose**: Displays a one-line summary of a manual page. • **Syntax**: **whatis command** • **Reference**: Chapter 4

alias	• **Purpose**: Creates or displays aliases, which are shortcuts for commands.
	• **Syntax**:
	  ○ **Create alias: alias name="command"**
	  ○ **Display aliases: alias**
	• **Reference**: Chapter 4

history	• **Purpose**: Displays the command history, showing a list of previously executed commands. • **Syntax**: **history [options]** • **Reference**: Chapter 12

7. Shell Builtins

This section provides a quick reference for commonly used shell builtins commands that are built into the Bash shell itself and always available, regardless of your PATH environment variable.

Command	Description
set	• **Purpose**: Sets various shell options, including those that affect how the shell interprets commands and handles errors. • **Syntax: set [options]** • **Common Options:** ○ **-e**: Exit immediately if a command returns a non-zero exit status (an error). ○ **-u**: Treat unset variables as an error. ○ **-x**: Enable script tracing, printing commands and their arguments before execution. ○ **-o option_name**: Enables or disables a specific shell option (e.g., **set -o noclobber** to prevent file overwriting). • **Reference**: Chapters 5, 19
export	• **Purpose**: Exports a variable, making it available to child processes (scripts or commands launched from the current shell). • **Syntax: export variable_name=[value]** • **Reference**: Chapter 11
source	• **Purpose**: Reads and executes commands from a file in the current shell environment. • **Syntax: source filename** • **Reference**: Chapter 11

read	• **Purpose**: Reads a line of input from the keyboard or standard input and assigns it to a variable.
	• **Syntax**: **read [options] [variable...]**
	• **Common Options**:
	  ○ **-p prompt**: Displays a prompt before reading input.
	  ○ **-s**: Reads input silently, without echoing it to the screen (useful for passwords).
	  ○ **-t seconds**: Times out after a specified number of seconds if no input is received.
	• **Reference**: Chapters 13, 15

trap	• **Purpose**: Sets up signal handlers for specific signals, allowing scripts to respond to events such as interrupts or termination requests. • **Syntax**: **trap command signals** • **Reference**: Chapters 18, 19
wait	• **Purpose**: Pauses script execution until specified background processes have completed. • **Syntax**: **wait [job_id ...]** • **Reference**: Chapter 18

Appendix B:
Glossary

This glossary provides clear and concise definitions of essential terms and concepts related to the Linux command line and shell scripting. Terms are arranged alphabetically for easy reference.

A

Absolute Path: (Chapter 1) A complete file or directory path that starts from the root directory (/) and specifies the exact location of the file or directory within the file system hierarchy. For example, */home/noah/Documents/report.txt* is an absolute path.

Alias: (Chapter 4) A user-defined shortcut for a command or a sequence of commands. Aliases allow you to create custom commands with shorter or more memorable names. For example, you could create an alias `ll` that executes the command `ls -l`.

Anchor: (Chapter 10) A special character in regular expressions that matches a specific position within the text, such as the beginning or end of a line. The two main anchors are:

- `^` **(caret)**: Matches the beginning of a line.
- `$` **(dollar sign)**: Matches the end of a line.

Argument: (Chapter 4) A value or piece of data passed to a command. Arguments can be filenames, directory names, options, or any other input that the command requires to perform its task.

Array: (Chapter 16) A data structure that can hold multiple values. Bash supports two types of arrays:

- **Associative Array**: (Chapter 16) An array where elements are associated with string keys, creating key-value pairs.
- **Indexed Array**: (Chapter 16) An array where elements are accessed using numerical indices, starting from 0.

Asynchronous Execution: (Chapter 18) A method of running processes where multiple tasks can execute concurrently, without waiting for each other to complete.

B

Background Process: (Chapter 10) A process that runs in the background, allowing the terminal to remain interactive and execute other commands while the process continues.

Bash Shell: (Chapter 1) The Bourne Again Shell, the most common shell used in Linux distributions. It provides a powerful command-line interface and a scripting language for automating tasks.

Bit Bucket (/dev/null): (Chapter 5) A special device file that discards any data written to it. It's often used to redirect unwanted output or error messages to effectively "silence" them.

Block Special File: (Chapter 3) A special file that represents a block device, such as a hard drive or a partition. Block devices handle data in blocks, allowing for random access to data.

Brace Expansion: (Chapter 2, 15) A shell feature that expands a pattern containing braces into a list of strings or numbers. For example, {1..5} expands to 1 2 3 4 5.

Branch: (Chapter 14) A decision point in the flow of execution within a script, typically implemented using an if statement, where the script chooses a different path based on the evaluation of a condition.

Broken Link: (Chapter 3) A symbolic link that points to a target file or directory that no longer exists.

Builtin Command: (Chapter 4) A command that is built into the shell itself, rather than being an external program. Builtin commands are always available, regardless of your PATH environment variable.

C

Character Class: (Chapter 10) A set of characters enclosed in square brackets ([]) in a regular expression. It matches any single character within the brackets.

Character Special File: (Chapter 3) A special file that represents a character device, such as a terminal or a printer. Character devices handle data as a stream of bytes.

Command: (Chapter 1) An instruction or set of instructions given to the shell to perform a specific task.

Command Line Interface (CLI): (Chapter 1) A text-based interface for interacting with the operating system by typing commands.

Command Substitution: (Chapter 13) A shell feature that allows you to capture the output of a command and use it as part of another command or assign it to a variable. The syntax is `$(command)`.

Comment: (Chapter 12) A line in a script that starts with a hash symbol (`#`) and is ignored by the shell. Comments are used to document code, explain its purpose, and improve readability.

Comparison Expression: (Chapter 14) An expression that compares two values and returns a boolean result (true or false) based on their relationship.

Conditional Execution: (Chapter 14) Executing a block of code only if a specified condition is met.

Constant: (Chapter 13) A variable whose value cannot be changed once it's assigned. Constants are often used for defining values that are fundamental to the script's logic or represent unchanging parameters.

Current Working Directory: (Chapter 1) The directory in which you are currently located within the file system.

D

Daemon: (Chapter 10) A background process that runs continuously, typically providing services or performing tasks without direct user interaction.

Debugging: (Chapter 19) The process of identifying and fixing errors, or bugs, in software or scripts.

Delimiter: (Chapter 8) A character or sequence of characters used to separate fields or columns in text data. Common delimiters include spaces, tabs, commas, and colons.

Device File: (Chapter 3) A special file that represents a physical or virtual device, such as a hard drive, a terminal, or a printer. Device files allow programs to interact with devices as if they were files.

Directory: (Chapter 1) A container within the file system that holds other files and directories. Directories are organized in a hierarchical structure.

E

Echo: (Chapter 12) A command that displays text or the value of a variable on the terminal.

Effective User ID (UID): (Chapter 6) The user ID that a process is currently using, which determines its permissions and access rights. The effective UID can be different from the real UID of the user who launched the process.

Error Handling: (Chapter 19) Techniques and code used to handle errors and exceptions that might occur during the execution of a script, such as invalid input, missing files, or runtime errors.

Escape Sequence: (Chapter 5, 12) A special sequence of characters used to represent control characters or special characters within a string.

Executable File: (Chapter 2, 12) A file that has execute permission, allowing it to be run as a program or script.

Exit Status: (Chapter 14) An integer value returned by a command or script when it finishes executing. A zero exit status usually indicates success, while a non-zero exit status indicates an error or a specific condition.

Expansion: (Chapter 13) A process where the shell replaces a variable name, command substitution, or arithmetic expression with its corresponding value or result.
- **Arithmetic Expansion**: (Chapter 13) Evaluates an arithmetic expression and replaces it with the result. The syntax is `$((expression))`.
- **Parameter Expansion**: (Chapter 13) Substitutes the value of a variable or performs operations on it. The syntax is `$variable_name` or `${variable_name}`.

Export: (Chapter 11) A command that makes a variable available to child processes, allowing them to inherit the variable and its value.

F

File Descriptor: (Chapter 5) A unique number assigned to a file or stream within a process. The standard streams (stdin, stdout, stderr) are associated with file descriptors 0, 1, and 2, respectively.

File Permission: (Chapter 2, 6, 17) Rules that determine who can access a file or directory and what actions they are allowed to perform (read, write, execute).

File System: (Chapter 1) A method of storing and organizing files and directories on a storage device, such as a hard drive or a USB drive.

File Type: (Chapter 2) A classification of files based on their contents and purpose, such as regular files, directories, symbolic links, and device files.

Filter: (Chapter 7) A command that processes data from standard input, performs some transformation on it, and sends the modified data to standard output.

Flow Control: (Chapter 14) Techniques used to control the order in which commands or statements are executed in a script, based on conditions or loops.

Foreground Process: (Chapter 10) A process that runs in the foreground of the terminal, taking control of the terminal and preventing other commands from being executed until it completes.

for Loop: (Chapter 15) A loop construct that iterates over a sequence of items, such as a list of words, a range of numbers, or the contents of a file.

Function: (Chapter 4, 18) A named block of code that performs a specific task and can be called from other parts of the script. Functions can accept arguments and return values, promoting code reusability and modularity.

G

Global Variable: (Chapter 18) A variable declared outside of any function, making it accessible from anywhere within the script, including inside functions.

Group ID (GID): (Chapter 6) A numerical identifier for a group of users. Files and directories can be assigned to a group, and users belonging to that group can have specific access permissions to those files.

H

Hard Link: (Chapter 3) A directory entry that points directly to a file's inode. Hard links create multiple names for the same file, sharing the same data blocks and inode.

Here Document: (Chapter 13) A way to embed a multi-line block of text within a script, redirecting it as input to a command.

Here String: (Chapter 13) A method for embedding a single-line string of text within a script, redirecting it as input to a command.

Hidden File: (Chapter 2) A file whose name starts with a dot (.), making it hidden by default when using the `ls` command. Hidden files are often used for configuration files and application settings.

Hierarchical File System: (Chapter 1) A file system organized in a tree-like structure, with the root directory at the top and directories branching out to hold files and subdirectories.

Home Directory: (Chapter 1) The personal directory for a user on a Linux system, where they store their files and configuration settings.

Hostname: (Chapter 1) A unique name that identifies a computer on a network.

I

`if` **Statement**: (Chapter 14) A flow control statement that executes a block of code only if a specified condition is true.

Index: (Chapter 16) A numerical value used to access a specific element in an indexed array. Array indices start from 0.

Inode: (Chapter 3) A data structure that stores information about a file, such as its size, permissions, ownership, and location of its data blocks on disk.

Input Redirection: (Chapter 5) Directing the input of a command to come from a file instead of the keyboard.

Interactive Mode: (Chapter 1) A mode of operation where the shell prompts the user for input and responds to commands typed by the user.

Interpreter: (Chapter 12) A program that reads and executes code line by line, such as the Bash shell.

J

Job: (Chapter 10) A process running in the background or foreground of a shell session.

Job Control: (Chapter 10) Mechanisms that allow you to manage and control jobs running in the background or foreground, such as suspending, resuming, and terminating them.

K

Key: (Chapter 16) A string value used to access a specific element in an associative array.

L

Line Continuation: (Chapter 12) Using a backslash () at the end of a line to indicate that the command continues on the next line.

Link Count: (Chapter 3) A value associated with a file's inode that indicates how many hard links point to that inode.

Linking: (Chapter 3) The process of creating multiple names for a file or directory using hard links or symbolic links.

Local Variable: (Chapter 18) A variable declared within a function, making it accessible only within the scope of that function.

Logical Error: (Chapter 19) A mistake in the logic of a script that causes it to produce incorrect results or behave unexpectedly.

Logical Operator: (Chapter 14) A symbol used to combine conditions in a logical expression, such as && (AND), || (OR), and ! (NOT).

Loop: (Chapter 15) A control structure that repeats a block of code multiple times, either a fixed number of times or until a specific condition is met.

M

Metacharacter: (Chapter 10) A special character in regular expressions that has a symbolic meaning and is used to define patterns, such as ., *, +, ?, and [ ].

Mount Point: (Chapter 15) A directory in the file system where another file system (e.g., a hard drive partition or a USB drive) is attached or "mounted."

N

Named Pipe: (Chapter 18) A special file that acts as a communication channel between processes, allowing them to exchange data. Named pipes work as FIFO (first-in, first-out) buffers.

O

Output Redirection: (Chapter 5) Directing the output of a command to a file instead of the terminal screen.

P

Parent Directory: (Chapter 1) The directory one level above the current working directory in the file system hierarchy.

PATH Environment Variable: (Chapter 4, 12) A system variable that contains a colon-separated list of directories where the shell searches for executable programs.

Pathname: (Chapter 2) A string that specifies the location of a file or directory within the file system, including the directory path and the file or directory name.

Pipeline: (Chapter 7) A sequence of commands connected by pipe symbols (|), where the output of one command is used as input for the next command.

Positional Parameter: (Chapter 12, 18) Special variables (e.g., $1, $2, $3, etc.) that hold the values of arguments passed to a script or function.

Process: (Chapter 10) An instance of a running program.

Process ID (PID): (Chapter 10) A unique numerical identifier assigned to each process by the operating system.

Process Substitution: (Chapter 18) A shell feature that allows you to treat the output of a command as if it were a file, using the syntax <(...) for standard output or >(...) for standard input.

Q

Quantifier: (Chapter 10) A special character in regular expressions that specifies how many times the preceding character or group should be matched.

R

Read Permission: (Chapter 2) The permission that allows a user or process to view the contents of a file or list the contents of a directory.

Redirection: (Chapter 5) A mechanism that allows you to change the source or destination of standard input, standard output, or standard error.

Regular Expression (Regex): (Chapter 10) A sequence of characters that defines a search pattern, commonly used for matching, searching, and manipulating text.

Relative Path: (Chapter 1) A file or directory path that specifies the location relative to the current working directory, without starting from the root directory.

Root Directory: (Chapter 1) The top-level directory in the file system hierarchy, denoted by a single forward slash (/).

S

Script: (Chapter 12) A text file containing a sequence of commands that the shell can execute as a program.

Shell: (Chapter 1) A program that provides a command-line interface for interacting with the operating system.

Shell Prompt: (Chapter 1) A symbol or set of characters that indicates the shell is ready to accept commands.

Shebang Line: (Chapter 12) The first line of a script, starting with #!, that specifies the interpreter used to execute the script.

Signal: (Chapter 10, 18) A software interrupt sent to a process, often used to terminate or control its execution.

Signal Handler: (Chapter 18) A function or code block that is executed when a specific signal is received by a process or script.

Source Code: (Chapter 4) The human-readable text of a program written in a programming language, which is then compiled or interpreted to create executable code.

Standard Error (stderr): (Chapter 5) The default output stream for error messages and diagnostic information.

Standard Input (stdin): (Chapter 5) The default input stream for commands, typically connected to the keyboard.

Standard Output (stdout): (Chapter 5) The default output stream for a command's normal output.

Sticky Bit: (Chapter 6) A special permission bit that, when set on a directory, restricts the deletion or renaming of files within that directory to the file's owner, the directory owner, or the superuser.

String: (Chapter 13) A sequence of characters, treated as a single unit of data.

Subdirectory: (Chapter 1) A directory contained within another directory.

Subshell: (Chapter 18) A separate instance of the shell that is created when running certain commands or pipelines.

Superuser (root): (Chapter 1) The administrative user account with the highest privileges on a Linux system.

Symbolic Link (Symlink): (Chapter 3) A special file that points to another file or directory, acting as a shortcut or alias.

Syntax Error: (Chapter 19) An error that occurs when the syntax of a command or script violates the rules of the shell's language.

Terminal Emulator: (Chapter 1) A program that provides a graphical interface for interacting with the command line.

T

Timestamp: (Chapter 2) Information associated with a file that indicates when it was last accessed, modified, or changed.

trap Command: (Chapter 18, 19) A shell builtin that sets up signal handlers, allowing scripts to respond to specific signals.

U

until Loop: (Chapter 15) A loop construct that repeats a block of code as long as a specified condition is false.

V

Variable: (Chapter 13) A named container that holds a value. Variables can be used to store data, perform operations, and make scripts dynamic and adaptable.

Version Control System: (Chapter 9) A system used to track changes to files over time, manage different versions, and facilitate collaboration among developers.

W

while Loop: (Chapter 15) A loop construct that repeats a block of code as long as a specified condition is true.

Wildcards: (Chapter 2, 10) Special characters used to match patterns in filenames or text. Common wildcards include:
- * **(asterisk)**: Matches any sequence of characters.
- ? **(question mark)**: Matches any single character.
- [ ] **(square brackets)**: Matches any single character within the brackets.

Write Permission: (Chapter 2) The permission that allows a user or process to modify the contents of a file or create, delete, and rename files within a directory.

Thank you for reading! I hope this book has empowered you to conquer the Linux command line.